ADDICTION &.
FOR BEGINNERS™

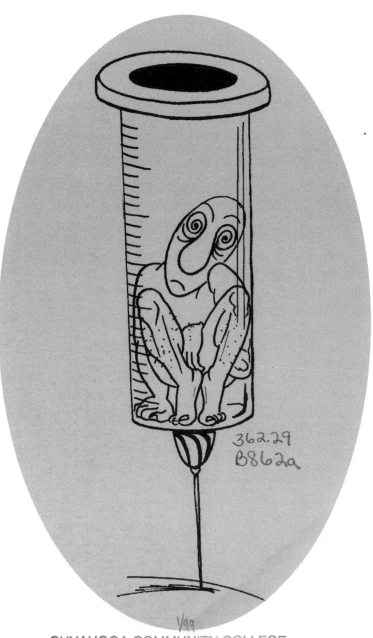

WRITERS AND READERS PUBLISHING, INC.

P.O. Box 461, Village Station
New York, NY 10014

Writers and Readers Limited
9 Cynthia Street
London N1 9JF
England

•

Text Copyright: © David Brizer
Illustrations © Ricardo Castañeda
Cover & Book Design: Terrie Dunkelberger
Cover Illustrations: Ricardo Castañeda

A Writers and Readers Documentary Comic Book
Copyright © 1996
ISBN # 0-86316-198-7 Trade
1 2 3 4 5 6 7 8 9 0

Manufactured in the United States of America

DEDICATION

To
Our
Parents

CONTENTS

ALCOHOL GAVE ME WINGS...

...AND THEN TOOK AWAY THE SKY.

—ANONYMOUS

ADDICTION & RECOVERY
FOR BEGINNERS™

WRITTEN BY DAVID BRIZER, M.D.
ILLUSTRATED BY RICARDO CASTAÑEDA, M.D.

Writers and Readers

Silence
is
the
enemy
of
recovery.

Seems like everyone's an addict these days.

Pills, alcohol, cigarettes, street drugs, sex, shopping, food, exercise—

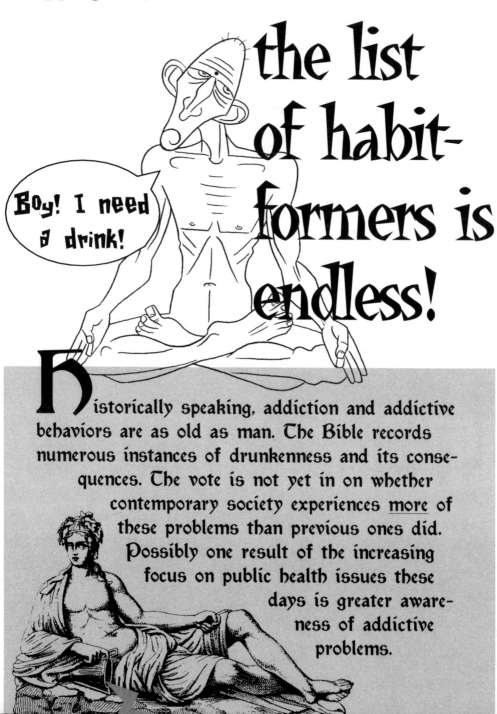

the list of habit-formers is endless!

Boy! I need a drink!

Historically speaking, addiction and addictive behaviors are as old as man. The Bible records numerous instances of drunkenness and its consequences. The vote is not yet in on whether contemporary society experiences _more_ of these problems than previous ones did. Possibly one result of the increasing focus on public health issues these days is greater awareness of addictive problems.

But... what IS "addiction"?

Addiction is any behavior that is repeated over and over despite significant negative consequences.

(Such as breathing smog-ridden air... freeway driving...or drinking polluted water? Not really. Most of us who do these things don't have much say in the matter. When we speak of addictions, we are referring to behavior that on some level is <u>elective</u>. We choose to drink or smoke or put dope in our veins (or at least we consciously made the choice the first few times we did so...)

Or to put it more scientifically, addictive behaviors feature <u>tolerance</u> and <u>withdrawal</u>.

Tolerance–

that's when it takes more and more to get the same effect as the very first time.

According to at least one biographer, a not unusual drinking day for writer Ernest Hemingway began with vodka and tequila, followed by Bloody Marys at noon, these succeeded in turn by Scotch and mixed drinks and untold amounts of wine to usher in the evening... .

*Let's take another crack at it_*

TOLERATING THIS AMOUNT OF ALCOHOL—AND REMAINING ABLE TO WRITE SOME OF THE MOST CELEBRATED PROSE OF OUR ERA—DEFINITELY QUALIFIES AS TOLERANCE.

Tolerance can be <u>metabolic</u>—as when your liver becomes more efficient at breaking down repeated doses of alcohol—

GEE—I WONDER WHY I CAN'T KEEP UP WITH YOU ANYMORE?

4

—**or** tolerance can be <u>cellular</u>, when the brain cells just don't get the same buzz they used to.

(WE'RE TALKING ABOUT DRUGS, & PHARMACOLOGY—NOT ABOUT YOUR MARRIAGE!)

SORRY, IT'S OVER. YOU JUST DON'T MOVE ME ANYMORE.

DRUG MOLECULE

BRAIN CELL

The physiologic basis of cellular tolerance remains a mystery. A more complete understanding of habituation on the micro level would be likely to lead to terrific advances in treatment and prevention.

Metabolic tolerance, on the other hand, is fairly well understood. <u>Liver enzymes</u> break down or <u>metabolize</u> nutrients, foreign substances and drugs. As the body is exposed to repeated doses of a drug, certain liver enzymes are induced...that is, they become more efficient at metabolizing the drug. This explains how a seasoned drinker can fly a B-32 (or write a novel) long after you or I have passed out under the table.

<u>Other famous owners of 'wooden legs'</u> include William Faulkner, F. Scott Fitzgerald, Janis Joplin, Edgar Allan Poe, John Steinbeck and let's not forget John Belushi (more properly described as having had a wooden nose...)

Withdrawal

can be relatively mild...

You call this mild?

THE GARDEN VARIETY SUNDAY MORNING HANGOVER IS NOTHING BUT A FORM OF MILD TO MODERATE ALCOHOL WITHDRAWAL.

...or can be devastatingly painful...sometimes to the point of seizures or even death.

You mean me?

Other terms for withdrawal are "crash," "jones," "coming down"... You get the picture.

COMING DOWN?

Withdrawal differs from one drug to another. The severity or discomfort or risk to health of withdrawal depends not only on the substance used, but on the frequency of use, the level of tolerance, the amount taken, and the time elapsed since last use.

Another term for addiction is

dependence

(as in chemical dependence.)

Dependence on a drug, or on an activity, is almost always accompanied by some degree of tolerance and withdrawal.

AS IMPORTANT AS IT IS TO HAVE A COMMON LANGUAGE WHEN DISCUSSING THESE MATTERS, IT'S ALSO IMPORTANT TO RECOGNIZE THAT THESE DEFINITIONS ARE NOT WRITTEN IN STONE.

Lesser forms of addiction have been termed

abuse.

SOUNDS LIKE ALMOST ANYTHING CAN BE ADDICTIVE—EVEN THIS BOOK!

HEAVEN

NORMAL HEAVY DRINKERS ALLOWED. BUT: ALCOHOLICS, ALCOHOL ABUSERS, AND PROBLEM DRINKERS GO BACK!

ADDICTION & RECOVERY FOR BEGINNERS

Make up your mind! Do I go in or not?

"Abuse," "dependence," "addiction" ...The experts have devoted fabulous amounts of time to clarifying these concepts. And the consensus still isn't in. Most workers in the addiction field prefer describing clients as "chemically dependent individuals" rather than as "addicts." The term "addict" has taken on many negative connotations over the years and obscures the fact that chemical use may be a disease rather than a moral short-coming.

The nervous system somehow **adapts** to repeated behaviors—and if these are particularly pleasurable, the brain is reluctant to give them up.

GEE! YOU MUST REALLY DIG THAT...

Neuroadaptation

describes more than tolerance and withdrawal. It is also the basis of the gradual diminution and eventual disappearance of our awareness of persistent sensory stimuli. Imagine what life would be like if we couldn't tune out the sensation of our clothing on our skin, or the constant rain of ambient noise on our eardrums! In _The Doors of Perception_, Aldous Huxley bemoaned our usual inability to appreciate things as they first looked or felt to us.

His solution?...

PSYCHEDELIC DRUGS!

But how do drugs <u>work</u>?

Psychoactive drugs (including alcohol) impact *neurotransmitters*, *neuronal receptors*, and *brain reward mechanisms*.

Mood, alertness, and thinking are influenced by—and maybe even depend upon—brain chemicals.

Hundreds of millions of brain cells (*neurons*) communicate with each other by means of highly organized relays and loops.

NEUROTRANSMITTERS LIKE DOPAMINE, NOREPINEPHRINE, AND SEROTONIN ARE THE CHEMICAL MESSENGERS THAT ALLOW BRAIN CELLS TO 'TALK' WITH ONE ANOTHER.

BREAK IT DOWN!!!

Neurotransmitters are released in the synaptic space between neurons and exert either an excitatory or an inhibitory effect on receptors of the next cell in line.

9

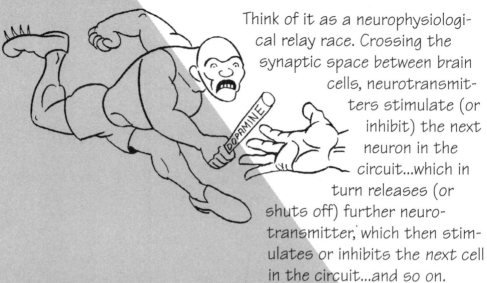

Think of it as a neurophysiological relay race. Crossing the synaptic space between brain cells, neurotransmitters stimulate (or inhibit) the next neuron in the circuit...which in turn releases (or shuts off) further neurotransmitter, which then stimulates or inhibits the next cell in the circuit...and so on.

Ultimately these neurotransmitters are taken back up into their neuron of origin and are either recycled for further use or are metabolized. This reuptake process effectively terminates the action of any given neurotransmitter molecule.

Some psychoactive drugs act directly on the receptor, while others block the reuptake mechanism, resulting in increased neurotransmitter presence in the synapse...and increased stimulation of neuron receptors.

I ONLY REGRET NOT HAVING MORE THAN 3 OR 4 LIVES TO GIVE TO MY SYNAPSES!

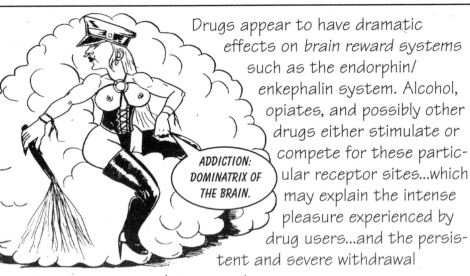

Drugs appear to have dramatic effects on brain reward systems such as the endorphin/enkephalin system. Alcohol, opiates, and possibly other drugs either stimulate or compete for these particular receptor sites...which may explain the intense pleasure experienced by drug users...and the persistent and severe withdrawal states users may later experience.

ADDICTION: DOMINATRIX OF THE BRAIN.

The brain is like a symphony—to sound right, all the different instruments must play together.

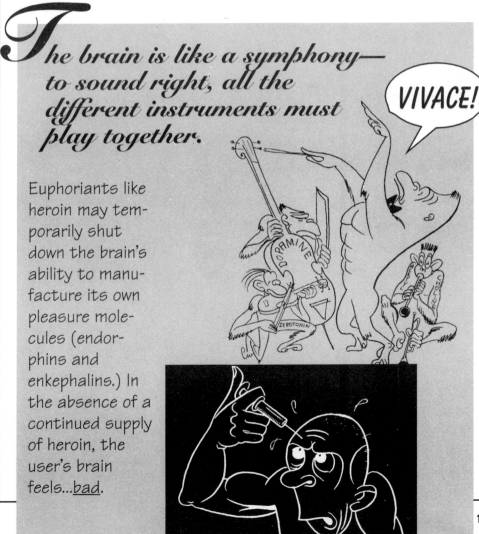

VIVACE!

Euphoriants like heroin may temporarily shut down the brain's ability to manufacture its own pleasure molecules (endorphins and enkephalins.) In the absence of a continued supply of heroin, the user's brain feels...<u>bad</u>.

OKAY, NOW THAT WE'VE SOLVED THAT MYSTERY, LET'S TRY THIS ONE ON FOR SIZE:

WHY do people use drugs?

Mr. Sherlock Holmes, known to rely on a seven-percent solution of cocaine hydrochloride to help him, umm—crack—his most difficult cases...

People use drugs:
Because it feels good...

...though not always! In a recent study one-third of psychiatric patients who used alcohol or street drugs reported that they felt <u>worse</u> after chemical use. When it comes to drug use, <u>changing</u> may be as important as <u>improving</u> the way you feel. 'Getting low' rather than 'getting high' may be the central drug experience for some...

> If merely 'feeling good' could decide, drunkenness would be the supremely valid human experience.
>
> William James, The Varieties of Religious Experience

people use drugs:

In order to feel that they belong...

Peer pressure can be the "gateway" experience for alcohol and drug use, particularly among adolescents. Prevention strategies aimed at the young seek to prevent the crystalization of identities around deviant behavior such as drug use: Drugs are <u>not</u> cool.

Or to just feel different...

Shy people, for example, may use drink or drugs to 'disinhibit' themselves, to make themselves more extroverted. The weak may feel strong, the dispirited outcast may become loquacious...after having "a few." Experiences can actually become "state-specific": a skill learned or practiced while high may become inaccessible during periods of sobriety (and vice versa.)

As a "social lubricant"...

We now know that certain individuals with social phobia—fear of interacting with others in public—use alcohol and other substances to "loosen up" in public. This strategy may work to a certain extent, but having to rely on alcohol every time one wants to shine socially can become PROBLEMATIC, or worse...

WANNADANCE?

To enhance their performance...

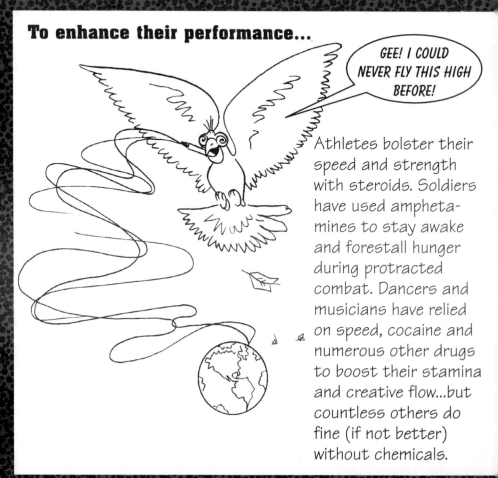

GEE! I COULD NEVER FLY THIS HIGH BEFORE!

Athletes bolster their speed and strength with steroids. Soldiers have used amphetamines to stay awake and forestall hunger during protracted combat. Dancers and musicians have relied on speed, cocaine and numerous other drugs to boost their stamina and creative flow...but countless others do fine (if not better) without chemicals.

Because their parents or other role models did...

As an experiment...

EENIE MEENIE MINIE MO...

Or in order to "self-medicate" painful emotions such as depression or loneliness or fear.

OH GOD! HOW DEPRESSING. I NEED A _TREAT_...

There is good evidence that alcoholism runs in families. Close relatives of alcoholics have a three to four times greater risk of alcoholism. Studies have also demonstrated higher likelihood of alcoholism in identical twins of alcoholics and among children of alcoholics who were raised in non-alcoholic homes. _This does not mean that children or relatives of alcoholics are fated to become alcoholics themselves._ Environment and other factors such as personality and intelligence strongly influence the individual's prognosis for presence or absence of addiction.

Consistent relationships between specific psychiatric disorders or personality traits and specific drugs of abuse have not been demonstrated. Nonetheless, there have been frequent reports of opiate use to 'self-medicate' rage and even psychosis (loss of contact with reality.)

> *Drunkenness is never anything but a substitute for happiness. It amounts to buying the dream of a thing when you haven't money enough to buy the dreamed-of thing materially.*
>
> —Andre Gide, *Journaux*

Drug use in the service of self-medication can set up a vicious cycle: someone who finds that they need to smoke a joint in order to accomplish a creative task may find their energy and inspiration levels further reduced by the marijuana.

In other words, Beethoven's *Fifth Symphony*...or the Normandy invasion on D-Day...were probably not created "under the influence."

Some artists, of course, swear by marijuana or booze. But probably more common are those who, taking a morning-after look at their midnight scribblings, find only an illegible or fuzzy-brained or downright laughable parody of inspiration.

Well, then... what exactly are drugs?

According to Webster, a **drug** is "any substance used as a medicine or as an ingredient in a medicine... ."

A **medicine** is defined as "any drug or other substance used in treating disease, healing, or relieving pain."

I JUST CAN'T GET ENOUGH!

A "DRUG" SUCH AS CRACK COCAINE NEITHER TREATS DISEASE, PROMOTES HEALING, NOR DOES IT RELIEVE PAIN.

Webster's definitions are overly narrow for another reason. People not only "drug" themselves with substances, but with...

- Shopping
- Gambling
- Sex
- Sports
- Television
- Money
- Work
- Religion

- Computers
- Pornography
- Power
- Hatred
- Travel
- Materialism
- Cars
- Relationships, etc., etc.

Every form of addiction is bad, no matter whether the narcotic be alcohol or morphine or idealism.

—C.G. Jung

Chemical intoxicants have been with us from the beginning.

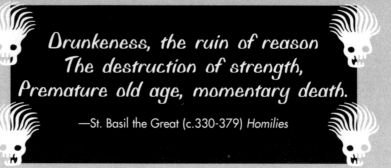

Ancient Greek, Roman, and Biblical sources document the not infrequent occurrence of drunkenness and its consequences in bygone times.

> *Drunkeness, the ruin of reason*
> *The destruction of strength,*
> *Premature old age, momentary death.*
>
> —St. Basil the Great (c.330-379) *Homilies*

There's a history to substance use. Alcohol and other drugs wax and wane in popularity, depending upon a number of factors, including availability, popularization by celebrities/role models, price, moral climate, legality, and more.

In the 1960s, recreational drug use was a significant part of the prevalent youth culture...use of marijuana and psychedelics became the norm for many. The 1990s have seen a return to the cultural sensibility of the 1920s, when illicit drug use was largely frowned upon and seen as an unfortunate habit of poor city dwellers, musicians, and others "on the fringe." By contrast, many drugs that are considered dangerous narcotics today were widely available over the counter in the late 19th century. The original Coca-Cola contained cocaine, as did a number of other nostrums and remedies available in drug stores to the general public without a doctor's prescription.

Right. But what do drugs DO?

DIFFERENT DRUGS HAVE DIFFERENT EFFECTS ON THE BRAIN AND THE BODY.

While some drugs such as alcohol and LSD have only one *psychoactive* (psychoactive = acting on the mind) compound, others such as marijuana have many active compounds. Not only that, but many drugs affect more than one type of neuronal receptor. This means that you can expect multiple physical and mental effects from most psychoactive drugs.

ONE WAY TO UNDERSTAND THESE IS TO **CLASSIFY** DRUGS.

THE DRUGGIE DECIMAL SYSTEM

VOL VIII

There's no single correct way to classify drugs. You can, for example, classify drugs by legal status (the U.S. Drug Enforcement Agency does this: cocaine, marijuana, heroin and LSD are all considered "Schedule I," i.,e., no recognized legitimate medical use... . The "compassionate" use of marijuana for treating chemotherapy-induced nausea has been killed by less kind and less gentle policymakers.) Drugs can also be categorized by structure (type of molecule) and by function (effect on the body.) The classification that follows is a functional one.

There's **ALCOHOL(s)**...

Including but by no means being limited to beer, near beer, lager, ale, stout, wine, still wine, new wine, port, schnapps, kir, aqua-vit, champagne, vermouth, scotch, rye, whiskey, absinthe, rum, ouzo, tequila, mezcal, sherry, brandy, cognac, amontillado, vodka, gin, sloe gin, etc., etc., etc., (HIC!)

IS THAT A HIP FLASK IN YOUR POCKET... OR ARE YOU JUST GLAD TO SEE ME?

You've got your **SEDATIVE/HYPNOTICS** (sleeping pills), including all classes and types of benzodiazepines and barbiturates... .

Rx PAIN-KILLERS & SEDATIVES

COCAINE HELPS ME UNWIND...

STIMULANTS, such as COCAINE, AMPHETAMINE, DEXEDRINE, PEMOLINE, CAFFEINE, NICOTINE, KHAT, EPHEDRINE, METHYLPHENIDATE, BIPHETAMINE, and others...

OPIATES, such as OPIUM, HEROIN, 'LAUDANUM', PAREGORIC, METHADONE, DILAUDID, PERCO-CET, PERCODAN, DEMEROL, DILAU-DID (tell us if you need more...)

COOL IT GEORGE...

HALLUCINOGENS, including LSD, MESCALINE, PEYOTE, CANNABIS, THC, HASHISH, ANGEL DUST, KETAMINE, PSILOCYBIN, MORNING GLORY SEEDS (now coated with a high-ly toxic chemical to discourage ingestion by recreationists), NUTMEG ("the Sailor's High"), and others...

...as well as **VARIOUS PRESCRIPTION PILLS** such as FIORINAL, DARVON, ELAVIL, DORIDEN, SOMA, COGENTIN, ARTANE, & YOU-NAME-IT...

and last but not least, probably the deadliest drug of all...

Smoking or chewing tobacco has been directly related to thou-sands upon thousands of death each year from cancers of the mouth, throat, and lungs; emphy-sema; chronic bronchitis; and heart disease. Cigarette smoking may aggravate hypertension and peptic ulcer disease.

21

It seems that the further one gets from the "natural" source of a substance—the more concentrated the active ingredient becomes—the greater the likelihood of trouble. This generalization may apply to all classes of intoxicants. For example (generally speaking), it may easier to induce severe paranoia with pure THC (tetrahydrocannibol, the active ingredient of marijuana or hashish) than with marijuana. Similarly, it may be easier to get "wasted" on hard liquor like vodka or scotch than on beer or wine.

Wine is a mocker, strong drink is raging; and whosoever is deceived thereby is not wise.
—Bible, Proverbs 20:1

ALCOHOL

MORE PUNCH?

ROCKY'S BAR
PALEOLITHIC PUNCH

Throughout the ages, men have come up with ingenious ways of transforming ordinary foodstuffs into...booze. And with even more ingenious ways of justifying it.

(WINE MAKING MAY BE THE WORLD'S OLDEST OCCUPATION.)

Wine—and inebriation—are frequently mentioned in the Bible, as well as in the writings of the ancient Greeks and Romans. Drunkenness became a major

XXX
VINTAGE:
2000 B.C.
MIS AM BOUTEILLE
AU SUMERIA

social problem in 18th-century England with the introduction of inexpensive gin... high alcohol blood levels could be reached quickly and cheaply with these new and powerful spirits...

Through the process of <u>fermentation</u>, yeast and other microorganisms convert grapes to wine...berries to gin...potatoes to vodka...and grain extracts into beer and whiskey.

I THINK THIS BREW NEEDS SOME MORE GUM...

Almost <u>anything</u> can be made into "brew"...

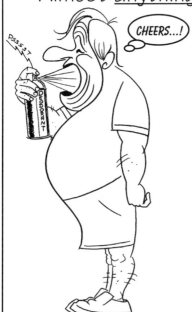

CHEERS...!

<u>Ethanol</u>, a simple two carbon-molecule, is the kind of alcohol we usually drink...

<u>Not all alcohols are the same</u>. Other alcohols—such as methanol (also known as wood, or grain, alcohol), or propyl (=rubbing) alcohol, are occasionally ingested...usually by accident...and usually with disastrous results.

FRENCH BLIND POETS' SOCIETY

Absinthe, once popular in France—especially among the visionary symbolist poets of the late 19th century—may have contained significant amounts of methanol ...and caused blindness and other types of brain damage among its devotees. Fermentation products of wormwood—the substance from which absinthe was brewed—may contain peculiar toxic and hallucinogenic compounds, which account for the drink's former popularity.

23

Man, being reasonable, must get drunk;
The best of life is but intoxication.

—Lord Byron, Don Juan II

The effects of alcohol are numerous and complex.

A small dose (=one or two beers, a glass of wine, or 1.2 ounces of hard liquor) causes a pleasant sense of warmth and relaxation.

Larger amounts lead to disinhibition (=loss of usual constraints on behavior), slurred speech, incoordination, and even unconsciousness.

The legal criteria for intoxication is a blood alcohol level (BAL) of 100 mg/ml (100 mg%) or greater. Those suspected of driving "under the influence" may be asked by police officers to give breath samples (alcohol is measurable on the breath) and/or to perform tests of coordination such as walking a straight line. BALs over 350 can lead to death.

Alcohol's sedative effect is transient. Alcohol-induced relaxation and sleep often gives way to racing pulse, dry mouth, anxiety, and insomnia. These are manifestations of rebound phenomena.

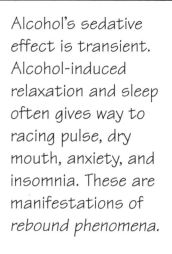

Alcohol is like love: the first kiss is magic, the second is intimate, the third is routine. After that you just take the girl's clothes off.
—Raymond Chandler,
The Long Good-bye

REBOUND?
THAT'S RIGHT, <u>REBOUND</u>. ALCOHOL, LIKE ANY OTHER PSY-CHOTROPIC DRUG, OBEYS WHAT I CALL <u>THE LAW OF DRUG KARMA</u>.

...WHICH IS?

WHAT GOES UP MUST COME DOWN...AND VICE VERSA. THAT IS, THE WITHDRAWAL EFFECTS OF ANY GIVEN DRUG ARE OPPOSITE IN NATURE TO ITS HIGH. THE CRASH FROM A STIMULANT INVOLVES FATIGUE, DEPRESSION, AND INCREASED APPETITE FOR FOOD...WHILE SEDATIVE WITHDRAWAL IS USUALLY CHARACTERIZED BY HYPERACTIVI-TY, INSOMNIA, AND ANXIETY.

REBOUND

The "Principle of Rebound" is ultimately democratic—it applies to *all* drugs of abuse and affects *all* drug abusers.

Here's how it works:

Whatever state a drug induces...the user can expect to experience the exact opposite when the particular drug wears off.

THE ONLY "CURE" FOR REBOUND IS ABSTINENCE...OR MORE DRUG!

So alcohol withdrawal—a hangover, the shakes, or at its most extreme, seizures or delirium tremens—result from an overactive brain, a nervous system in overdrive.

DTs, or *delirium tremens*, is a life-threatening condition precipated by withdrawal from repeated use of large amounts of alcohol. Visual hallucinations, fever, and high blood pressure may accompany DTs and require immediate medical attention.

Alcohol's effects on memory can be...dramatic.

Those who drink too much may lose partial or complete recall of where they were and what they were doing while drinking (alcoholic blackout.)

Chronic heavy drinkers may develop permanent brain damage; persistent memory problems; Korsakoff's psychosis (where the alcoholic "confabulates," or makes up identities and facts to fill in the gaps in his or her impaired memory); acute confusional states (Wernicke's encephalopathy); and chronic hallucinations (alcoholic hallucinosis).

WHAT DID YOU SAY YOUR NAME WAS...?

> *An alcoholic is someone you don't like who drinks as much as you do.*
>
> —Dylan Thomas, in *Dictionary of 20th Century Quotations*

Rarely, one or two drinks can lead to a dramatic loss of self-control (**paradoxical disinhibition**). This reaction can include severe agitation and assaultiveness in ordinarily placid peaceful types.

But then again there are those who feel "fine" even with blood alcohol levels in the stratospheric (or potentially lethal) range. The explanation for this is <u>tolerance</u>. Those who are accustomed to regularly consuming large amounts of alcohol metabolize it more quickly and often "stand up to" its intoxicating effects better than teetotalers or habitually light drinkers.

QUESTION: IF YOU HAD TO CHOOSE, WOULD YOU RATHER HAVE YOUR 747 FLOWN BY AN ALCOHOLIC PILOT WITH A MODERATELY HIGH BLOOD LEVEL OF ALCOHOL AND A STEADY HAND—OR BY AN ALCOHOLIC PILOT WHO HADN'T HAD A DRINK IN TWO DAYS?

Curiously, many believe that alcohol is an effective hypnotic (sleep medication). Untrue! While the initial effect of small to moderate amounts is relaxation, the body and brain experience rebound within four to six hours. Rebound from alcohol includes rapid heart rate, excess perspiration, insomnia, and anxiety. There's no way to get around "Drug Karma": whatever a substance does to you when you're high...you can expect the opposite set of reactions as it leaves your system... .

And what is # ALCOHOLISM?

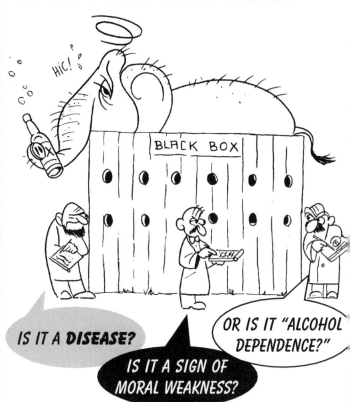

IS IT A **DISEASE**?

IS IT A SIGN OF MORAL WEAKNESS?

OR IS IT "ALCOHOL DEPENDENCE?"

Dissension and controversy among the experts are not unique to the alcoholism field. Psychiatrists have been arguing for years about diagnoses...to the point where the "official" manual for psychiatric diagnosis (*The Diagnostic and Statistical Manual*) goes through regular periodic revisions as research, and further dissension and controversy, help consolidate "data."

No animal ever invented anything so bad as drunkenness—or so good as drink.

—G.K. Chesterton, *All Things Considered*

Patterns of drinking differ greatly from person to person (and from culture to culture.) In general, alcoholic (or "problem") drinking appears as binges, which may occur regularly on weekends, (or at any other time); or as regular daily ("maintenance") drinking, necessary for getting through the day.

First you take a drink, then the drink takes a drink; then the drink takes you.

—F. Scott Fitzgerald, quoted in Jules Feiffer's *Ackroyd*

E.M. Jellinek (*The Disease Concept of Alcoholism*) described "species" of alcoholism. So-called "Gamma" alcoholism, common in America, is characterized by loss of control: once the alcoholic starts drinking, he cannot stop. This in contrast to the typical alcoholic drinking pattern in France, where alcoholic drinkers simply cannot abstain, but do not necessarily go on benders like their alcoholic counterparts in the U.S.

Alcoholics drink although they "know better."

They drink despite the presence of emotional (or physical or vocational or family) difficulties that have been caused by drinking.

They keep drinking even after "going on the wagon" once or twice or many times (i.e., "I have no trouble quitting—I've done it a thousand times.")

THIS ONE AND ANOTHER ONE AND ANOTHER, AND ANOTHER, AND ANOTHER ... ARE FOR YOU

BEER

I'M ON THE WAGON!!!

I've made it a rule never to drink by daylight and never to refuse a drink after dark.

—H.L. Mencken

As the saying goes: for the alcoholic,

"a thousand drinks are never enough, and one is too many."

Some observed cultural differences may be instructive.

Where drinking is ritualized—where children see wine used regularly and moderately at meals—alcoholism is not rampant. Taking wine with the family at table ("Italian model") is a highly <u>social</u> activity...as opposed to solitary drinking of potent grain spirits("Irish model"), which promotes isolation, guilt, rejection...and more drinking!

I'M NOT LIKE THOSE "ANONYMOUS" GUYS - I DRINK PUBLICLY.

Alcoholism runs in families. Children of alcoholics are much more likely to become alcoholics than children of non-alcoholics— even when they are raised apart from their alcoholic parents.

YOU MEAN I'M DOOMED?

NOT AT ALL! ALCOHOLISM, LIKE MOST HUMAN BEHAVIORS, IS **MULTIFACTORIAL** IN ORIGIN. PROBLEM DRINKING—OR HEALTHY DRINKING—RESULTS NOT ONLY FROM GENETIC PREDISPOSITION, BUT FROM THE INTERPLAY OF PERSONAL STRESS LEVEL, TEMPERAMENT, COPING STYLE, AND PRESENCE OF RESOURCES SUCH AS EDUCATION, JOB, FRIENDS, AND FAMILY.

"Adult Children of Alcoholics" is a quasi-diagnostic label that has been applied to the millions who have had to grow up with an alcoholic parent. To the extent that the alcoholic household was characterized by abuse, neglect, and other forms of violence, the 'ACOA' is said to carry extra emotional baggage such as depression, anxiety, tendency toward addiction and unhealthy relationships.

Though not included in the DSM, "co-dependence" is considered by many in the addiction field to be a necessary if not invariable concomitant of living with (or under) an alcohol-dependent person. Bear in mind that both the ACOA and the co-dependency concepts have been criticized for lack of scientific rigor and overinclusiveness.

ALCOHOLISM, SCHMALCOHOLISM... WHAT'S WRONG WITH HAVING A FEW?

PLENTY. AMONG DRUGS OF ABUSE, ALCOHOL MAY BE ONE OF THE DEADLIEST.

I DON'T KNOW ABOUT THAT...

Who could have foretold, from the structure of the brain, that wine could derange its functions?
Hippocrates (c. 460-377 BC)

Alcoholism's cost to society is staggering. The annual cost in terms of injury, disability, and accidents is estimated at well over $100 billion for the U.S. alone.

DID WE MAKE IT TO THE FORTUNE 500?

GO AHEAD, MAKE MY DAY.

Alcohol and drug use is involved in at least 50% of all violent crimes.

Drunkenness is simply voluntary insanity.
—Seneca (c. 4BC-65AD)

Some of this reflects the direct effect of alcohol and other drugs on behavior. For example, alcohol is well-known for its *disinhibiting* effects, its ability to make people more impulsive and less concerned about consequences of their immediate actions. (Users of crack cocaine may be quite promiscuous.) Indirect effects of drug use up to and including violent crime are mediated by the users' perpetual need for more money for more drugs. An entire subculture—of which murderous violence is a not infrequent concomitant—has grown up around the use and sale of hard drugs like heroin and cocaine. And as the drug culture becomes increasingly associated with poor undereducated urban youth, so does the correlation between drug use and crime.

Unlike heroin, whose facilitating effect on crime appears to be indirect, alcohol has a primary *disinhibiting effect*, which can result in impaired judgment, loss of impulse control, and violence.

> *Drunkenness is temporary suicide. The happiness that it brings is merely negative, a momentary cessation of unhappiness.*
>
> —Bertrand Russell, *The Conquest of Happiness*

The personal toll on the alcoholic is no less dramatic.

TO KNOW ALCOHOLISM IS TO KNOW MEDICINE...

...SINCE ALCOHOL AFFECTS EVERY ORGAN SYSTEM IN THE BODY.

LETS TAKE A SPIN...

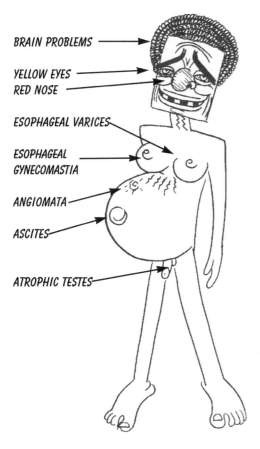

BRAIN PROBLEMS

YELLOW EYES
RED NOSE

ESOPHAGEAL VARICES

ESOPHAGEAL
GYNECOMASTIA

ANGIOMATA

ASCITES

ATROPHIC TESTES

sequence of destructive changes to other organ systems.

Blood supply to and from the cirrhotic liver, for example, backs up, resulting in congestion of the spleen...hemorrhoids...and *esophageal varices*, which can rupture without warning and cause fatal hemorrhage.

AND THAT'S
NOT ALL.

The medical consequences of alcohol use are widespread and range from benign to fatal. *Alcoholic liver disease*, for example, may begin as an inflammation of the liver (hepatitis) that can resolve on its own or progress... With continued use of alcohol, the inflamed liver may begin to scar—*cirrhosis*—which then results in a whole

The damaged liver no longer manufactures blood proteins effectively, so that alcoholics may suffer massive swelling of the abdomen and extremities. As a result of impaired liver metabolism of sex hormones produced in the body, male alcoholics may undergo feminization, with increased development of breast tissue and change in pubic hair pattern.

35

Alcoholic liver disease—the final stage of which is cirrhosis—is no picnic.

End-stage alcoholics can hemorrhage fatally...hear voices or see things... develop convulsions...develop ulcers...all at the drop of a hat.

Alcoholics who smoke are ten times as likely as nonalcoholics to develop cancers of the head and neck.

Alcohol's diuretic effect can result in the washout of drugs like lithium, resulting in subtherapeutic blood and body concentrations of drug.

And alcohol can interfere with the action of prescribed medication...and amplify the effect of sedatives to the point of unconsciousness, coma, or even death.

This is an example of pharmacological synergism, where alcohol potentiates the effects of drugs like barbiturates and benzodiazepines on the nervous system.

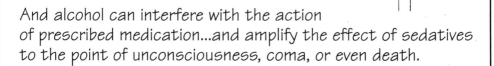

36

Chloral hydrate has been used for decades for its tranquilizing and hypnotic (= sleep-inducing) effects. Anyone who's ever been "slipped a mickey" knows how potent the combination of alcohol and chloral can be...

Barbiturates have been around for decades too. Barbiturates used to be the only show in town, at least as far as sleeping pills and tranquilizers were concerned.

Short-acting barbiturates such as amobarbital (Amytal) and secobarbital (Seconal, "reds") have a rapid onset of action, wear off relatively quickly, and have high potential for abuse.

Longer acting barbiturates such as phenobarbital are used as anticonvulsants and in the treatment of alcohol withdrawal.

...and then there was

VALIUM...

Valium (diazepam), when first introduced to the public in the 1950s, was heralded as a safe and effective treatment for anxiety... . Soon enough doctors were widely pre-scribing it for a host of indications, including sleep problems, "bad nerves," "the blues," and any num-ber of other complaints... .

Researchers soon refined the product, creating dozens of other benzodiazepine drugs that differed from Valium in potency and duration of action.

Valium spin-offs include *Xanax* (alprazolam), *Ativan* (lorazepam), *Klonopin* (clonazepam), *Restoril* (temazepam), and *Halcion* (triazolam.)

These differ from each other mainly in rapidity of onset and in *half-life* (duration of therapeutic effect).
Diazepam (Valium), clonazepam (Klonopin), and chlor-diazepoxide (Librium) have longer half-lives than their molecular kissing cousins Ativan (lorazepam) and Halcion (tria-zolam.) The longer-acting benzodi-azepines are favored as anticonvul-sants and detoxifying agents, while drugs like Ativan and Halcion are preferred as "sleepers" because they work rapidly and wear off by morning...

SOUNDS GOOD TO ME... WHAT'S THE PROBLEM?

When used appropriately—for the *brief* treatment of insomnia or anxiety disorders—there usually is no problem.

However, continued use of these medications, particularly at high doses and particularly among addiction-prone individuals, can lead to dependence.

Apothecary, n. The physician's accomplice, undertaker's benefactor and grave worm's provider.

—Ambrose Bierce, *The Devil's Dictionary*

REMEMBER WHAT WE SAID ABOUT DRUG REBOUND?

Anxiety or panic or insomnia can be as bad or worse once you stop your benzodiazepines.

Unfortunately, some individuals who have been taking "benzos" for years find that they have an enormous amount of difficulty getting off these drugs for good. As the dose of their medication is progressively reduced they may find themselves plagued by intense insomnia, anxiety, and tension.

IS THERE NO WAY OUT?

39

FORTUNATELY, YES...

Other treatments for anxiety or insomnia may be as effective or even more effective than Valium-like drugs...or may pick up where the benzodiazepines leave off.

For example, many doctors treat anxiety problems with non-addictive antidepressants these days. Benzodiazepines can be helpful for the temporary treatment of anxiety and panic, but in most cases should be given in conjunction with an antidepressant (such as Prozac, Paxil, Zoloft, Wellbutrin, Effexor and others). The antidepressant may eventually be all that's needed to prevent moderate to severe anxiety.

Researchers are scrambling to identify the sites of action of benzodiazepines and other drugs in the brain. Work has been progressing on the identification of specific benzodiazepine receptors in the brain; these appear to be linked to the effects of GABA (gamma amino butyric acid, yet another neurotransmitter molecule in the central nervous system).

Benzodiazepines and barbiturates are *cross-tolerant* with alcohol (i.e., regular heavy drinkers may find that they require relatively greater amounts of benzodiazepines or barbiturates to achieve a therapeutic effect.) Because of this cross-tolerance, benzodiazepines and barbiturates can be used to treat alcohol withdrawal. Typical detoxification regimens from alcohol involve gradually tapered doses of Librium or Valium administered over the course of five or more days.

Other sedative/hypnotics can have even higher potential for abuse and addiction than the benzodiazepines...including *Miltown* (meprobamate), *Doriden* (glutethimide), *Placidyl* (ethchlorvynol), and *Quaalude* (methaqualone, no longer available in the U.S.) And unlike the benzodiazepines, which are relatively difficult to overdose on (when taken alone, that is), severe intoxication with these drugs can be lethal.

TOO MANY OF THESE CAN REALLY SEND YOU TO DREAMLAND...FOREVER.

WITHOUT MY VALIUM, MILTOWN, PLACIDYL, LIBRIUMS, FIORINAL, AND DALMANE I'M JUST A BUNDLE OF RAW NERVES...

(Don't laugh! One reason a glass of warm milk may help induce sleep is that milk is rich in *tryptophan*, an amino acid that becomes the neurotransmitter *serotonin* in the brain. Psychopharmacologists believe that serotonin is involved [among other things] in regulation of the sleep cycle.)

Why some prefer "down" heads, while others prefer to be as awake and alert as possible, is not fully understood.

Studies of correlations or matches between personality types and preferred drug of abuse are inconclusive. (This may be another "chicken or egg" dilemma, namely, Which came first? The "personality type" or the substance use? We do know that continued use of chemical intoxicants leads to alterations in behavior and personality.)

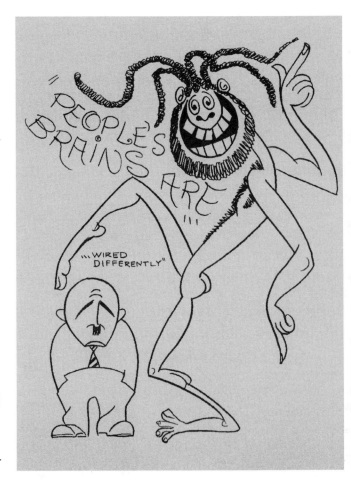

"PEOPLE'S BRAINS ARE...WIRED DIFFERENTLY"

Of course, when things get a little *too sleepy*—there are always

STIMULANTS!

DON'T EVEN BOTHER SAYING "GOOD MORNING" TO ME UNTIL I HAVE MY FIRST CUP!

Stimulants of one kind or another have been in use for centuries.

For hundreds of millions of Westerners, starting the day without a bracing cup of java would be...unthinkable. In Africa, some enjoy *khat*, a stimulant herb that can be taken as a tea.

Molecularly speaking, many stimulants (amphetamine, methamphetamine, *Benzedrine*, others) bear an uncanny resemblance to neurotransmitters found in the brain.

The human mind is capable of excitement without the application of gross and violent stimulants; he must have a very faint perception of its beauty and dignity who does not know this.

—William Wordsworth, *Lyrical Ballads*

It is possible that these drugs are "mimic neurotransmitters" and gain access to brain cell receptors by dint of their structural similarity to neurotransmitters like dopamine and norepinephrine.

QUICK! WHAT DO YOU SEE HERE?

43

AMPHETAMINE

NEURON

CATECHOLAMINES

Amphetamine causes neurons to release extraordinary amounts of catecholamines like norepinephrine and dopamine into the synaptic space...resulting in excess and prolonged activation of neurons.

Researchers once considered the possibility that certain forms of severe mental illness (such as schizophrenia) were caused or were accompanied by excess levels of amphetamine-like compounds in the brain. This was the so-called *amphetamine model of psychosis*. Although this was never borne out, we do know that amphetamine intoxication can resemble some psychotic states. (Paranoid delusions, hypervigilance, and excess motor activity are common to both.) We also know that *antipsychotic* medications block *dopamine receptors*; dopamine receptor blockade alleviates both psychosis and stimulant intoxication.

"Speedballing"—simultaneous use of heroin and cocaine—is an attempt to suppress some of the physical and mental hyperactivity (including paranoia) that often accompanies cocaine use alone. Others drink alcohol to take the edge off a jaw-grinding cocaine high.

Relative to other drugs, cocaine's history is recent, but colorful. Cocaine is extracted from the leaf of the coca plant, *Erythroxylon coca* (it is extremely difficult to synthesize in the lab). Coca is indigenous to the mountainous terrain of South America (Columbia, Peru). In the 19th century, cocaine (like many other psychoactive drugs) was sold over the counter as a component of various patent medicines. Cocaine was one of the ingredients in the original (not 'Classic'!) *Coca Cola* beverage...although this was left out in later versions of the drink. Sigmund Freud championed the drug for a time, proposing it as a cure for addiction to opiates...in recent years, with the introduction of more potent forms of the drug, its potential and actual destructive nature is more fully appreciated.

Cocaine interferes with the normal reuptake/degradation of catecholamines...once again resulting in excess and prolonged activation of neurons...

...eventually leading to neurotransmitter depletion and...

YOU CAN'T GET SOMETHIN' FOR NUTHIN'...

CRASH!!!

REBOUND, THAT IS, THIS TIME IN THE FORM OF EXTREME FATIGUE AND HUNGER AND DEPRESSION.

Stimulant withdrawal, though not directly life-threatening, can significantly interfere with functioning and lead to extreme depression. (Doctors have had some success using antidepressants to treat states of stimulant-induced neurotransmitter depletion.)

AM I REALLY THAT PREDICTABLE?

This helps to explain patterns of stimulant use. The typical cocaine sniffer goes on a binge...which is followed by a period of remorse and fervent resolutions to *Never pick up again*...succeeded by rebound fatigue, apathy, and depression...and more use.

Or the cocaine user will enjoy a return to normal functioning and take this as an indication that he can use again with impunity.

45

The cycle is much more extreme among those who inject or smoke cocaine.

Coke is available either as the hydrochloride— sniffable, snortable, and generally available to the body through the mucous membranes—

OR AS FREEBASE.

Freebase, which is usually smoked, is prepared by some simple home chemistry...

ANYONE CAN DO IT.

Compared with snorters, smokers of cocaine experience a boost in blood level that is much higher and much more rapid. The crash is much more painful too.
Freebase or crack users go on "runs" that can last several hours. Or several days.

The run ends only when there is (i) no more drug; (ii) no more cash; or (iii) no more user. As any *habitué* will tell you, the crack crash is...well, let's call it **DEVASTATING**, and leave it at that. Users will go to almost any extreme to prevent this psychic nosedive...and "chasing the dragon" can have disastrous financial or medical results.

Drug dealers achieved a marketing coup when they realized that freebase could be packaged and sold as small smokable pellets — crack — which, at ten dollars a vial, seems like a cheap enough high...

BUT TAKE ANOTHER LOOK!

The extremely rapid boost in cocaine blood levels following inhalation of crack or injection of cocaine is accompanied by extreme euphoria...

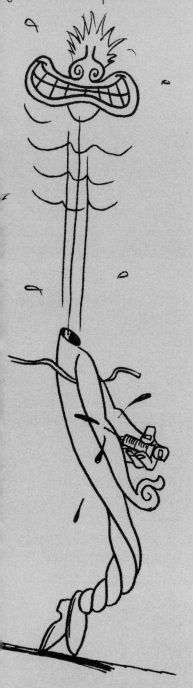

But as any user can tell you,

THE CRASH IS JUST AS AWESOME.

Blood levels of smoked or injected cocaine drop very quickly, and crack cocainists describe withdrawal as *one of the worst feelings in the world*. So that one vial of crack immediately leads to another—and another and another and another... Crack users have been known to go through *thousands of dollars'* worth of drug during a binge.

And that's not all. At the end of a crack "run," users are absolutely desperate to get their hands on more. Not uncommonly the run will end with users scouring the floors and carpets on their hands and knees for more pebbles to smoke. Users also resort to prostitution ("sex for drugs") and dealing to get more cash for drugs.

While high, cocainists and amphetamine *afficionadoes* are **very, very alert... hypervigilant...**

AND SOMETIMES **DOWNRIGHT PARANOID.**

The hyperalert hyperactive brain tries to explain its perceptions. Sensory misperceptions—*illusions*—can give way to hallucinations and delusions, given the proper set and setting. (Sounds suspiciously like psychosis?)

The tense paranoid state can become so uncomfortable that users drink or take sedatives or opiates in an effort to "chill out." Some even present themselves to hospital emergency rooms for care.

...Then again, it all depends on exactly *which* stimulant is being used and *who's* using it and *how*. Some individuals have a "maintenance" pattern of (usually low grade) stimulant use that allows them to live and work and interact without major problems. Stimulants such as methylphenidate (Ritalin) are routinely prescribed for thousands of patients with attention deficit disorder—and most of these individuals do not require dosage boosts with time.

PHYSICAL CONSEQUENCES OF STIMULANT USE CAN INCLUDE CARDIAC ARRYHYTHMIAS, LUNG DAMAGE, STROKE, HEART ATTACKS, CONVULSIONS, AND DEATH.

WHAT'S WRONG WITH A NICE JOINT INSTEAD?

Nothing! Pot and mushrooms and acid are the royal road to self-knowledge! (That's what people were saying back in the 1960s, at any rate... Interesting how different people at different times have such contrasting views about and uses for psychoactive drugs.)

In the 1960s, a youth counterculture based on love, self-awareness, and freedom from material pursuits flourished.

Dr. Timothy Leary, a Harvard psychologist, became one of the leaders of the "Turn on, tune in, drop out" movement of the sixties. The hope of many at the time was that chemically-induced introspection would heal many of our personal and societal ills. Today, Dr. Leary enjoys Sunday television football and beers with his pals at his Beverly Hills digs. He recently responded to an interviewer's question about "The White Light" by commenting that as far as he knew, he had paid his electric bill on time.

Dr. Timothy Leary
~ 1960 ~

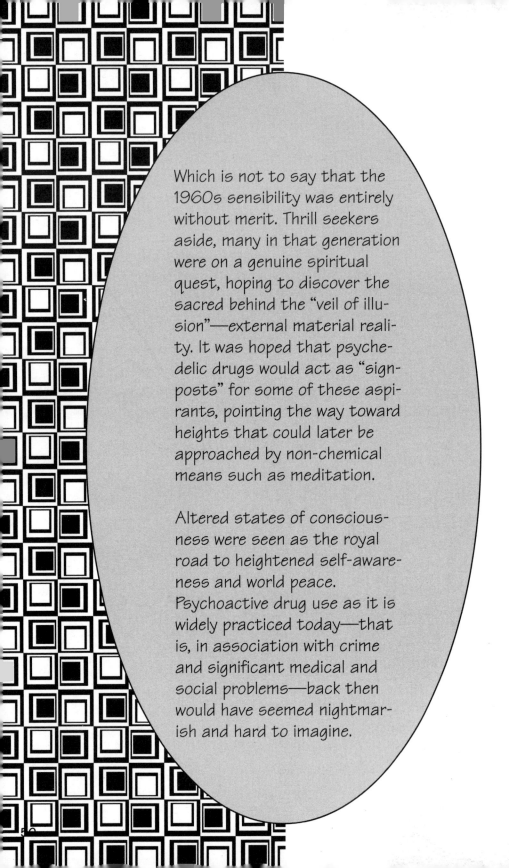

Which is not to say that the 1960s sensibility was entirely without merit. Thrill seekers aside, many in that generation were on a genuine spiritual quest, hoping to discover the sacred behind the "veil of illusion"—external material reality. It was hoped that psychedelic drugs would act as "signposts" for some of these aspirants, pointing the way toward heights that could later be approached by non-chemical means such as meditation.

Altered states of consciousness were seen as the royal road to heightened self-awareness and world peace. Psychoactive drug use as it is widely practiced today—that is, in association with crime and significant medical and social problems—back then would have seemed nightmarish and hard to imagine.

Hallucinogens

MARIJUANA, harvested from the flowering tops of the *Cannabis sativa* plant, grows in many parts of the world and has been with us for millenia. Marijuana is commonly smoked as a cigarette—a "joint"—or rolled up cigar fashion (a "blunt.")

HASHISH (*Cannabis* resin), a more potent derivative of marijuana, typically comes in bricks, pieces of which are smoked in pipes or mixed with marijuana or tobacco in cigarettes.

Users may experience a sense of detachment, of bliss, or an intense appreciation of colors and tastes and sounds...may end up rolling on the floor in laughter...or find themselves consumed by eye-popping paranoia.

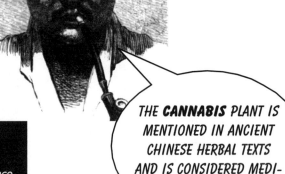

> No drug, not even alcohol, causes the fundamental ills of society. If we're looking for the sources of our troubles, we shouldn't test people for drugs, we should test them for stupidity, ignorance, greed, and love of power.
>
> —P.J. O'Rourke, Give War a Chance

THE **CANNABIS** PLANT IS MENTIONED IN ANCIENT CHINESE HERBAL TEXTS AND IS CONSIDERED MEDICINAL IN SOME CULTURES.

The active ingredient in marijuana, delta-9-THC (tetrahydrocannibinol), found use for some time as an anti-nausea agent in patients undergoing cancer chemotherapy. With drug laws that are less kind and less gentle than ever, this "compassionate use" of marijuana is no longer permitted.

THC is the purified psychoactive compound in marijuana and may be taken orally or smoked. Taken as THC, it is much more potent than marijuana itself...

...and therefore may be more likely to induce

anxiety, panic,

and

paranoid

reactions.

As with all other psychoactive drugs, the subjective marijuana experience depends to a large extent on the user's set (attitude and expectations of the user) and setting.

Which means, among other things, that marijuana (and all other drug) experiences are intimately linked to the surroundings in which they occur. A joint smoked on a balmy day at a Grateful Dead concert will feel very different from the same joint smoked under fire in Vietnam!

Research has confirmed these impressions. Subjects given doses of caffeine, for example, were asked to identify the drug they had taken...and the subjects' guesses varied widely, depending upon the expectations they brought with them to the study.

Compared with drugs like alcohol and nicotine, which are well-known killers, marijuana is a benign, relatively harmless indulgence.

Why the public and legislators react so strongly to these substances is a matter for speculation. [The Drug Enforcement Agency lists marijuana and LSD as "Schedule I" drugs: not to be prescribed under any condition. Prison sentences for those caught using and/or selling these are often stiff. In 1992, the U.S. Public Health Service announced the end of "compassionate use" of THC for treating cancer chemotherapy-induced nausea.] Yet statistics indicate that "legal" drugs like alcohol and tobacco cause overwhelmingly greater amounts of sickness and death in our society. Perhaps people are frightened by the prospect of "mind-expanding drugs." Better to drink, better to narrow the limits of our vision...

BUT IS "POT" SAFE?

DEPENDS ON WHAT YOU MEAN BY "SAFE."

WHAT WE CAN'T OR WON'T SEE CAN'T HURT US....

ON THE OTHER HAND...

...on the other hand, chronic—as in months or years—marijuana use can cause lung damage or problems with learning and motivation.

Since the vast majority of pot smokers inhale deeply (cigarette smokers tend to restrict their smoke intake to the upper airway), chronic and/or heavy marijuana smokers may be at risk for bronchitis, emphysema, and cancer.

DMT, LSD, MDA, and mescaline are much more potent hallucinogens than marijuana.

(DMT—*dimethyltryptamine*— is another of those curious neurochemical analogues, tryptamine being the precursor molecule of the brain transmitter serotonin.)

Microgram [=one millionth of a gram] amounts of these cause intense hallucinations, delusions, and synaesthesiae.

SYNAE-WHOZIT?

Synaesthesiae. That's when sensations cross boundaries, as in (if you can imagine it) "hearing" colors or "smelling" sounds...

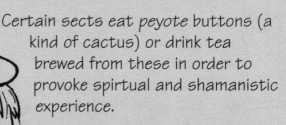

<u>Psilocybin</u> is derived from the Amanita muscara plant, or "magic mushroom."

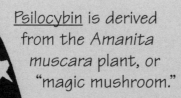

Certain sects eat peyote buttons (a kind of cactus) or drink tea brewed from these in order to provoke spirtual and shamanistic experience.

The drug experience is culturally and historically bound. What seems to mainstream America like a self-indulgent and dangerous exercise in drug experimentation has functioned in other societies as a rite of initiation. The visions and insights gained from drug-induced experiences have been highly treasured in cultures other than our own.

Mescaline, the purified hallucinogenic derivative of the peyote cactus, is usually available in powdered form and can be taken orally. Aldous Huxley described his intense mescaline experiences in *The Doors of Perception.*

> AND EVEN IN OUR OWN, AT LEAST AT ONE POINT.

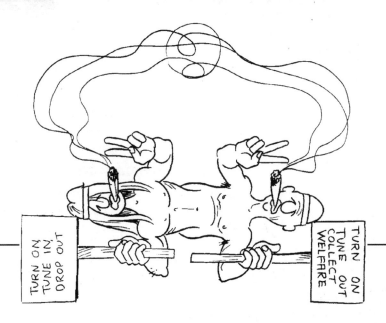

In the 1960s, an entire generation of young Americans were encouraged to find inner meaning and peace with the help of these drugs. "Dropping acid" and "dropping out" were reactions to a society that was perceived as pathologically focused on material gain. The 1960s represented a generation's call to spiritual arms.

Although first touted as "mind-expanding," the psychedelic drugs can cause serious mental disturbances, including paranoia, frightening hallucinations, panic attacks, and depression. Those whose trips become overwhelming may require sedatives until the acute reaction is over. (Unanticipated visits to the emergency room are particularly frequent with *phencyclidine* (PCP)— see pg 58.)

CAN YOU GET ME BACK TO...YESTERDAY?

LSD (lysergic acid diethylamide), DMT, and "designer drugs" like MDA and MDMA are produced in the laboratory. Too often, the "laboratory" is located in someone's basement...catastrophes due to poor quality control have been known to occur on occasion.

DMT, MDA AND MDMA HAVE IMPORTANT STRUCTURAL SIMILARITIES TO NATURALLY OCCURING NEUROTRANSMITTERS AND HAVE PROFOUND EFFECTS ON THESE.

Psychiatric researchers were fascinated by the 'psychotomimetic' (=ability to mimic psychoses) properties of drugs like LSD. Some hypothesized that schizophrenics had DMT-like compounds in their brains. Efforts to treat schizophrenia by dialysing or washing toxic substances out of the blood of afflicted patients failed.

One batch of designer drugs was contaminated with a powerful neurotoxin... several of those who were unlucky enough to be on the receiving end of these ended up with severe intractable movement disorders, which in at least one case proved to be fatal.

WHY ON EARTH ARE THEY CALLED DESIGNER DRUGS?

BECAUSE THEY WERE DESIGNED TO SLIP THROUGH LOOPHOLES IN THE LAW. AT ONE TIME, DRUGS LIKE ECSTASY (MDMA) AND MDA WERE NOT BANNED BY ANY FEDERAL STATUTES.

Homemade synthetic drugs are by no means confined to the psychedelic category. Analogues of fentanyl (a potent opioid painkiller) and of meperidine (another narcotic) have been produced in clandestine laboratories.

BOTH MDA AND MDMA HAVE BEEN SHOWN TO BE NEUROTOXIC AT DOSAGES COMMONLY TAKEN BY RECREATIONAL USERS. MDMA HAS BEEN PARTICULARLY POPULAR AMONG COLLEGE STUDENTS.

A word of caution to would-be basement chemists: Structural similarity of molecules does not imply similar toxicity levels. 7-chloroamphetamine, for example, is quite similar on a molecular level to amphetamine, but acts as a potent neurotoxin when given to experimental

LSD has been used as an aid in psychotherapy.

MDA ("the love drug," so-called because of its reputation for dissolving inhibitions and promoting instant "togetherness") has been touted as a safe and effective aphrodisiac.

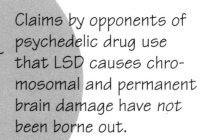

SOUNDS GOOD? THEN SEE THE PREVIOUS PAGE!

Claims by opponents of psychedelic drug use that LSD causes chromosomal and permanent brain damage have *not* been borne out.

Its name notwithstanding, **ANGEL DUST** (phencyclidine, PCP) can be one helluva trip.

PCP is very similar to *ketamine*, which is used as an anaesthetic for animals (and as a recreational drug for humans, who call it "Special K").

These drugs affect numerous brain receptors and organ systems, producing a variety of responses ranging from euphoria to hypertension to convulsions; they can cause a persistent and sometimes very treatment-resistant form of psychosis.

60

PCP is usually smoked (dusted on tobacco or marijuana leaves). Some unsuspecting users of doctored weed have ended up in emergency rooms for treatment of severe anxiety or depressive states. Some users develop persistent psychosis (hallucinations, delusions, loss of contact with reality) following exposure to one or more doses of the drug.

PCP USERS TEND TO BE **POLYSUBSTANCE** USERS AND ABUSERS...

—"garbageheads" who seem willing to take almost anything to change the way they think and feel.

Granted, it's an ugly name. But those who are indiscriminate in their use of powders and potions, of smokables and injectables, really do treat themselves "like trash."

Sometimes changing the way you feel is far more important than the direction or type of change, or what you have to take to get there...

For art to exist; for any sort of aesthetic activity or perception to exist, a certain physiological precondition is indispensable: intoxication.

—Friedrich Nietzsche, *Twilight of the Idols*

Unlike hallucinogens, **OPIATES** like morphine and heroin (=diacetylmorpine) lull users into a state of inaction and placidity. "Dopers" are rarely if ever violent as a *direct* result of opiate use—criminal behavior usually results from a desperate need for money for more drug.

The doors of perception gently close shut...

HERE! GET REALLY STONED ON THESE SEEDS TONIGHT AND CALL ME NEXT WEEK.

Opium, derived from the poppy plant (indigenous to the Far East), was used as a medicinal agent as long as 3500 years ago.

Paregoric, a mild opiate derivative, is prescribed for colicky babies to this day.

Opium smoking became a major social problem in China in the 18th and 19th centuries.

Morphine was not isolated from opium until 1806...and its use by injection did not become common until the late 19th century. The progression to intravenous heroin didn't take place until the early 20th century. As with other drugs, the movement toward more potent drugs, taken by more direct routes of administration (i.e., by injection), resulted in greater damage to both the individual and to society at large.

Morphine and morphine derivatives (codeine, hydromorphone, others)—as well as synthetic "opioids" like Fentanyl, Methadone, and buprenorphine—find legitimate use as analgesics (= painkillers.)

Fact is, opiates and opioids are the most powerful painkillers known. Problem is, the "mental" and "physical" (who knows where one ends and the other begins?) pain relief afforded by the opiates is so reinforcing that some find themselves craving the drug to alleviate the pain of opiate withdrawal.

Opiate dependence is a curious thing. Although many heroin users rapidly escalate their daily intake (to the point where obtaining and using the drug becomes the exclusive focus of their lives), others are able to "maintain" themselves on a stable dose for months and even years. This has been the case for some users of *methadone* (a long-acting opioid which is taken as a substitute for heroin), as well as for many who take opiates chronically for pain syndromes.

And not all opiate enthusiasts become career addicts.

Only a minority of the thousands of GIs who used heroin in Vietnam remained dependent on the drug following their return home.

Opiate. An unlocked door in the prison of identity. It leads into the jailyard.
—Ambrose Bierce, *The Devil's Dictionary*

Naturally occurring painkillers, called *endorphins* and *enkephalins*, fit in lock-and-key fashion into *opioid receptors* in the brain.

Endorphins are released in stress and pain situations—they are the body's response to pain. Certain behaviors including strenuous exercise, fasting and possibly meditation may also cause release of these *endogenous opioids*...which explains how activities like running or dieting can become so reinforc-ing (rewarding.)

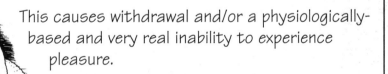

QUIET DOWN THE OPERA SEÑOR TENOR. THE LADY IS TALKING...

CAN WE TALK!

OPIATE

RECEPTOR

When exogenous (=from out-side the body) opiates are taken regularly, the brain's feedback mechanism shuts down endorphin (= "endogenous morphine") man-ufacture and release.

This causes withdrawal and/or a physiologically-based and very real inability to experience pleasure.

COMING WITH ME?

Without additional doses of heroin or methadone, the user goes into withdrawal...which, as any addict can tell you, *is no picnic.*

It's likely that the vicious and physiologically determined cycle of drug use, withdrawal, and further (escalating) drug use described here for opiates is also operative for other substances of abuse.

If you think dope is for kicks and for thrills, you're out of your mind. There are more kicks to be had in a good case of paralytic polio or by living in an iron lung. If you think you need stuff to play music or sing, you're crazy. It can fix you so you can't play nothing or sing nothing.
—Billlie Holiday, in *Lady Sings the Blues* (with William Duffy)

Heroin (=diacetylmorphine) effects last four to six hours, so the heroin addict finds him or herself needing a hit three to four times a day. It's easy to see how drug procurement and consumption can come to completely dominate the user's life style. Compulsive drug use becomes a full time 24 hour-a-day seven day-a-week job...

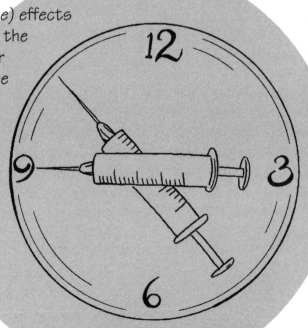

Opiate withdrawal can include shivering, diarrhea, vomiting, severe insomnia, anxiety, and depression...which, though lasting for days, is generally not life threatening. Nonetheless, opiate withdrawal is so unpleasant that users will go to extremes—

INCLUDING PROSTITUTION, ROBBERY, AND MURDER

—to get another fix.

And that, unfortunately, is *not* where it ends. Following *acute* (up to one week) withdrawal, users often go on to experience *subacute* or protracted withdrawal syndromes. These can last for months at a time and are characterized by persistent insomnia, depression, and anxiety.

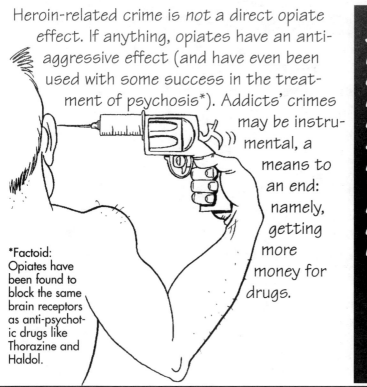

Heroin-related crime is *not* a direct opiate effect. If anything, opiates have an anti-aggressive effect (and have even been used with some success in the treatment of psychosis*). Addicts' crimes may be instrumental, a means to an end: namely, getting more money for drugs.

*Factoid: Opiates have been found to block the same brain receptors as anti-psychotic drugs like Thorazine and Haldol.

Junk is the ideal product...the ultimate merchandise. No sales talk necessary. The client will crawl through a sewer and beg to buy.
—William Burroughs, *Naked Lunch*

Two strategies for breaking the cycle of opiate addiction and crime are legally sanctioned opiate prescriptions (as in Great Britain) and methadone maintenance. Methadone is a long-acting once-a-day substitute for heroin. Thousands of individuals receive daily doses at methadone maintenance treatment programs across the U.S. Some (but not all) MMTP clients are able to function adequately in families and in jobs because their opiate dependence has been stabilized: their dosage requirements do not escalate, they are able to avoid other drugs of abuse, and methadone usually has no adverse long-term effects on health.

Withdrawal isn't the *only* problem that opiate habitués face... . You *can* have too much of a good thing!

Heroin is purer than ever these days (unless diluted, or "stepped on"). Which means that unsuspecting users, hoping to achieve ever higher highs, may inadvertently overdose, ending up as patients on the *Eternal Care Unit...*

Another problem has to do with contaminated needles and syringes. In their haste to get a fix, intravenous drug users may share "works" with one another...and may also get to share blood-borne diseases like Hepatitis and AIDS.

Methadone mainte-nance and publicly funded needle exchange programs target this preventable spread of potentially lethal infection.

Drug users—particularly intravenous drug and crack cocaine users— tend to practice unsafe sex. This may be for plea-sure or in the service of procuring more drug ("sex for drugs"). Education efforts aimed at high-risk populations may help lower the spread of sexu-ally transmitted diseases.

HOW ABOUT _INHALANTS_? THEY'RE SAFE ENOUGH, AREN'T THEY?

NO...

...although some are definitely worse than others. On a spectrum of dangerousness, nitrous oxide ("laughing gas") is probably less harmful than some of the volatile solvents used recreationally. These include shoe polish, cleaning fluid, and model airplane glue, typically emptied into and sniffed from a paper bag.

Like most other drugs, these, too, have a history.

The Victorians enjoyed ether and nitrous "frolics" before either of these agents found legitimate use as anaesthetics.

Substances currently used to obtain a cheap high—glue, gasoline, aerosol propellants—can cause severe and even life-threatening damage to the liver, kidneys, and brain.

AMYL NITRATE ("poppers"), an inhalant contained in a glass vial that is cracked open and sniffed, produces an intense rush (related at least in part to its ability to cause precipitous drops in blood pressure). Amyl enthusiasts tout its orgasm-enhancing effects... A typical setting for amyl nitrate use is in sex clubs and other places where promiscuity and "anonymous" sex are practiced with dizzying frequency.

Butyl nitrate is available over (or under) the counter in small bottles and is also inhaled for the intense rush and supposed orgasmic potentiation that it provides.

QUICK! GET ME THE AMYL NITRATE. I'M READY FOR LOVE...

Frequently available and abused inhalants also include spray paint, hair sprays, nail polish remover and cleaning fluid. A recent survey demonstrated a prevalence of nearly 20% of inhalant use among high school students.

Users may experience euphoria, excitement, slurred speech, and incoordination.

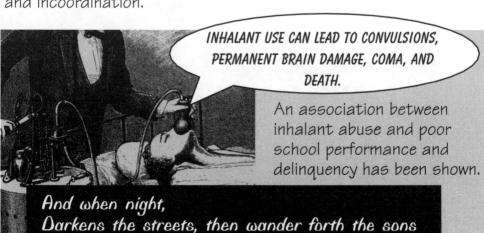

INHALANT USE CAN LEAD TO CONVULSIONS, PERMANENT BRAIN DAMAGE, COMA, AND DEATH.

An association between inhalant abuse and poor school performance and delinquency has been shown.

*And when night,
Darkens the streets, then wander forth the sons
Of Belial, flown with insolence and wine.*

—John Milton, *Paradise Lost*

71

Caffeine, the most widely used mood-altering drug in the world, can cause caffeinism (caffeine intoxication) as well as a *bona fide* withdrawal syndrome following cessation of moderate to heavy use.

The caffeine withdrawal syndrome includes decreased energy, fatigue, headache, and increased irritability, typically peaking 24 to 48 hours after the last cup.

Caffeinism can feature any or all of the following: stomach upset, palpitations, dizziness, trouble sleeping, agitation, anxiety, and restlessness.

These days, of course, its easier than ever to get a good caffeine fix. Coffee bars (*Tired? Get wired!*) have become a regular feature of urban life...and caffeine-loaded 64 ounce sodas (gulp!) seem to be a permanent feature of suburban convenience stores. Imagine if illegal drugs ever became equally accessible.

PUT THAT IN YOUR MUG, AND SIP IT!

Nicotine, on the other hand, is completely harmless...

HARMLESS, THAT IS, UNLESS YOU TAKE INTO ACCOUNT THE **HUNDREDS OF THOUSANDS OF DEATHS EACH YEAR FROM CANCER, HARDENING OF THE ARTERIES, AND CHRONIC LUNG DISEASE THAT WE NOW KNOW ARE DIRECTLY RELATED TO USE OF TOBACCO PRODUCTS...**

Tobacco use accounts for <u>400,000 premature deaths</u> each year in the U.S., compared with some 100,000 attributable to alcohol. Annual deaths directly related to use of illicit drugs on the other hand have been estimated at some 20-30,000...

DON'T BE ALARMED. I'M FILTERED...

Under the pressure of the cares and sorrows of our mortal condition, men have at all times, and in all countries, called in some physical aid to their moral consolations—wine, beer, opium, brandy or tobacco.
—Edmund Burke, *Thoughts and Details on Scarcity*

73

Tobacco wasn't always this harmful. Pre-Columbian Indians who chewed or smoked tobacco in pipes certainly did not have the widespread and severe lung problems that beset modern cigarette smokers.

Less potent forms of drugs taken by less effective routes of delivery (i.e., chewing tobacco leaves instead of inhaling tobacco smoke, or drinking beer instead of distilled spirits) are less likely to cause serious harm.

LUNGS ARE OK — BUT MY GUMS ARE KILLING ME...

The comparison with illicit drug use is again instructive.

Although there may be 3 million American users of illicit drugs, cigarette smokers are estimated at **50 million** and heavy drinkers at **10 milllion**.

Based on these numbers, you can easily work out the comparative degree of damage for yourself...

I'M NEXT...

One-third of Americans over the age of twelve smoke.

WHY?

Why do people smoke? (Read no further. Please turn to page 77 for an explanation of why people use drugs. Any and all of these apply to smokers.)

Nicotine has been shown to be a very powerful reinforcer in animals (who will press levers in cages to get it). Nicotine has been shown to be a very powerful reinforcer in humans, who will go to great lengths (even walk a mile!) to smoke. Cigarettes can reduce anxiety, increase alertness, and become associated in smokers' minds with powerful rewards (reinforcers) like decreased anxiety, increased alertness, post-meal satisfaction...and post-coital bliss.

The average one pack-a-dayer takes 70,000 puffs over the course of a year... good luck trying to quit anything you do that often!

Like coffee drinkers, smokers who quit may find themselves bedeviled by a definite withdrawal syndrome, characterized by fatigue, irritability, anxiety, and decreased alertness. Only one-third of those who quit remain abstinent after one year.

The good news is that there is some evidence that educational efforts help prevent non-smokers from picking up the habit. We also have evidence that cigarettes act as a "gateway" drug—young people who use illicit drugs are more likely to be smokers than those who don't.

Those who change to lower nicotine brands may find themselves simply smoking more cigarettes per day. Some have achieved abstinence with the help of nicotine or clonidine patches...and millions have just quit.

THERE! MAYBE NOW I WON'T FINISH THIS CIGARETTE...

Theories of Addiction

Behavioral
Social Learning
Dynamic
Biologic
Self-medication

People have been grappling with the question—*Why do people use drugs?*—for some time now. A related question—*How is it that some people can use drugs recreationally while others become addicts?*—is just as difficult to answer.

BEHAVIORAL models explain drug use and other addictive behaviors on the basis of *conditioning and reinforcement.*

We know from experiments with laboratory animals that drug highs are extremely reinforcing—a rat will work to the point of starvation, exhaustion, and even death to press a lever that causes cocaine to be released into its brain. Rats and people then become conditioned, that is, they associate previously "neutral" environmental cues (music, sex, the dealer's neighborhood) with the drug effect and start craving the moment they are exposed to these deeply embedded "reminders" of the drug.

I SAY "NO" BUT MY BRAIN SAYS "YES"!

JUST SAY NO

SOCIAL LEARNING theory highlights the effect of *social influences*—such as peer pressure, cultural and family values (or absence of these)—on the acquisition of addictive behavior.

Alcoholics Anonymous and others emphasize the importance for recovering addicts of avoiding "people, places, and things."

Exposure to drug cues may not only provoke conditioned responses but may instill values and behaviors that need to be "unlearned" at subsequent points in time.

MAYBE WE CAN PUT THEM ALL IN ORPHANAGES...!

Everything one does in life, even love, occurs in an express train racing toward death.

To smoke opium is to get out of the train while it is still moving.

It is to concern oneself with something other than life or death.

BIOLOGICAL explanations cite neuroadaptation as the key process in addiction. The brain somehow adapts to repeated exposure to alcohol (or drugs or shopping sprees or gambling or promiscuity)...and then experiences states of deprivation, or *withdrawal*, when the original stimulus is withheld. Specific changes in brain cell receptors and brain blood flow may accompany states of intoxication and withdrawal.

*SO, WHAT **NOW**? WHAT??*

SELF-MEDICATION hypotheses posit a relationship between painful mood states such as anxiety and depression and the use of drugs. According to this theory, people drink or drug in order to change or improve the way they feel. This is a circular process, since withdrawal from substances ends up aggravating the baseline mood problem.

But none of these models adequately explains how or why Person X becomes an addict—and Person Y does not. Addiction may result from the impact of numerous facilitating factors—availability of drugs, peer pressure, desire to escape from ordinary states of mind—upon what has been called an "addictive personality."

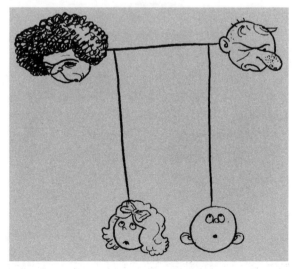

Research has demonstrated some heritability for alcoholism. Studies of twins and of children of alcoholic parents raised by non-alcoholic parents show that there is some genetic transmission of alcoholism. Children of alcoholics: don't despair! Other work strongly suggests that individual factors such as intelligence and specific character traits can override or make up for a strong genetic predisposition to alcohol problems.

In the 1960s, thousands of American soldiers used cheap and potent heroin while stationed in Vietnam. Yet, of these, only a tiny fraction remained addicted upon their return to the U.S.

Addiction results from the interplay of mind set (=personality, expectations) and setting (=environment). In the more familiar, vastly safer and more supportive setting of home, these soldiers no longer needed to "self-medicate" with opiates and other drugs.

This is likely to be the case for most adolescent 'experimental' drug use as well. During the teen and early adulthood years, defying authority and trying new and possibly dangerous experiences are the norm. Later in life, such behaviors come to be considered inappropriate or deviant and are discarded by the majority.

According to the self-medication hypothesis, people use drugs to escape painful states of mind. As attractive as this theory may be, it fails to explain why some people with depression (or anxiety or other mental problems) use drugs while others don't. There's another problem too. It also turns out that different people with the same mental problems (depression, anxiety, others) prefer to use *different* types of drugs—with variable effect on how they ultimately feel!

Users do tend to have drugs of choice. But let's not oversimplify matters. Many users follow a carefully sequenced ritual that may involve use of two or more drugs, such as cocaine and alcohol. Many users take great pains to "titrate" their drug experience. A little cocaine may go a long way toward re-alerting an individual whose alcohol or marijuana intake has made them feel overly sedated or sloppy.

If people *do* self-medicate anger, depression, and anxiety with alcohol and drugs, then you'd expect the mentally ill to be self-medicating **BIGTIME**...and they do!

In recent years, clinicians and policy-makers have become increasingly and painfully aware of a sizable segment of the mentally ill population who habitually abuse drugs. Their problems are so substantial that we give this group their very own name:

MICAS (MENTALLY ILL CHEMICAL ABUSERS; ALSO KNOWN AS **'DUAL DIAGNOSIS'** OR **'DOUBLE TROUBLE'** PATIENTS.)

SOME FEEL BETTER, SOME DON'T, AND SOME FEEL WORSE. GO FIGURE!

MICA problems—related to homelessness, need for repeated hospitalizations or other types of medical care—are very costly and very difficult to solve. Persons with both mental illness and substance use disorders tend to do more poorly in treatment than those with mental illness alone. It is not unusual for MICAs to require repeated hospital admissions for detoxification, episodes of psychiatric illness and other life crises. Those who treat MICA patients are uniquely challenged to skillfully combine interventions for addictive and psychiatric problems.

For example: MICA individuals may "blame" their substance use on their mental illness. Or they minimize their mental illness, ascribing most or all of their problems to the drugs they use. Those who treat these problems must appreciate the complex interactions that occur between substance use and mental disorders (if they are to be effective as treatment providers.) **MICAs need strong doses of education in order to successfully master their double affliction.**

DRUG COMBOS:

"OH WHAT A TANGLED WEB WE WEAVE WHEN FIRST WE PRACTICE TO DECEIVE."

BET YOU CAN'T JUST SMOKE ONE...

What about this idea that using one drug (the "gateway" drug) makes using another more likely?

Careful study of individual drug "careers" reveals that in fact many addicts do progress from cigarettes and/or alcohol and/or marijuana to harder drugs like coke and heroin.

"Gateway" drugs are associated with later use of more dangerous drugs. Concern about this fuels some of the arguments against legalization of marijuana (cigarettes and alcohol notwithstanding...)

STAIRWAY TO NIRVANA →

I'd hate to be a teetotaller. Imagine getting up in the morning and knowing that's as good as you're going to feel all day.
—Dean Martin, in *Filmgoer's Companion* (Leslie Holliwell, ed.)

83

"POLY" WANTS A CIGARETTE, AND A DRINK, AND A PILL, AND A "CRACKER"...

These days, consistent use of only a single drug by an individual is more often the exception than the rule. Poly (=many) substance use takes many (!) forms. Drinkers like to punctuate their drinking with cigarettes—and report that drinking numbs their mouths and throats so they end up smoking much more than they do when not drinking.

Similarly, those who chill out their coke highs with drink usually find that they can handle much more alcohol when using cocaine. A recent study demonstrated that the alcohol withdrawal experienced by cocaine users is actually milder than that suffered by those who drink but do not drug. A big problem in recent years has been cocaine use by those receiving methadone maintenance.

Sedative and particularly opiate users like to "titrate" their highs, using just enough coke, for example, to keep them alert and awake but not "wired." "Speedballs" (intravenous heroin plus cocaine) are an example of this.

Marijuana smokers occasionally get more than they bargained for, in the form of "dust" (angel dust, PCP), which can be sprinkled on pot and smoked along with it.

Polysubstance users may acknowledge problems with one favored drug but insist that they have absolutely no problem with one or more others (see *Treatment*, below.) Those who are struggling to quit one particular drug often find themselves substituting others for their drug of choice.

This can be a particularly thorny issue when it comes to pain management. Those recovering from alcohol or drug dependence should work closely with their doctors if and when they require medication for pain control, since many analgesics are highly abusable and can trigger a return to full blown addiction.

ONCE TICKLED, THE NEURONS OF ADDICTS WANT MORE!

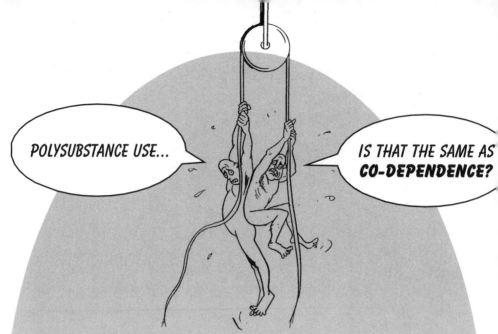

POLYSUBSTANCE USE...

IS THAT THE SAME AS **CO-DEPENDENCE?**

Not really. *Co-dependence* refers to a set of misery-making behaviors that often arise in those whose loved ones have serious addiction or other life problems. Those who live with alcoholics or otherwise dysfunctional people may come to feel responsible for—and helpless and frustrated and depressed by—the other's problems.

The term is of relatively recent origin and is frequently used by those recovering from addiction. The claim that co-dependence is a disease—a disease deserving aggressive treatment efforts—is highly controversial.

Co-dependence isn't the only recent addition to the lexicon of "Recovery." "ACOA" is an "Adult Child of an Alcoholic"...ACOAs are thought by some to be a clinically recognizable group with a more or less homogenous group of symptoms including (you guessed it!) co-dependence, depression, and anxiety.

CO-ADDICTION REFERS TO DEPENDENCE UPON TWO OR MORE SUBSTANCES.

ATHLETE ADDICTS & POWER JUNKIES

You wouldn't know a steroid addict if you saw one.

WHO, ME?

Steroid abusers try to enhance their physique, athletic performance and sense of well-being with these drugs...and in the short run, they succeed.

Anabolic (=body-building) steroids like testosterone are hormones that influence metabolism, growth, sex drive, and aggression. Users find that anabolic steroids help them acquire additional muscle mass or improved speed or endurance.

FEMINIZATION OF MEN
MASCULINIZATION OF WOMEN
DEPRESSION
ANXIETY
VIOLENCE
DRUG USE
LIVER DISEASE

Athletes take them in order to perform stronger, better, and faster. Problems with these compounds (aside from the fact that they are addicting, and that users can suffer major abstinence symptoms) include their potential for serious negative consequences such as increased likelihood of heart disease, stroke, and cancer; shrinking testicles; increased aggressiveness ("'roid rage"); and balding.

Users typically take steroids in cycles, or runs, lasting from one to five months, with steroid-free intervals in between. Steroids are taken orally, by injection, or by both routes. Because of the proliferation of steroid abuse in athletic circles, most professional leagues (and the Olympics) routinely run urine tests to detect the presence of steroids.

EATING DISORDERS

People have been over- and undereating since the Dawn of Thyme. It's only in recent years that extremes of eating behavior have been, umm, *widely* thought of as disorders or addictions.

It's unclear whether or not there has been an actual increase in the incidence of these problems in recent years. Some speculate that our culture's emphasis on appearance— <u>thin</u>, of course, being ideal—coupled with the "commoditization" of women results in higher frequency of eating disorders.

These problems may be harder to treat than alcohol or drug dependencies since

 food is ubiquitous, and

 a hell-bent course of self-starvation is difficult to disrupt.

BULIMICS live to eat (rather than eat to live.) Food is instrumental for them, serving as reward, as relief, as release from all the cares and worries of life.

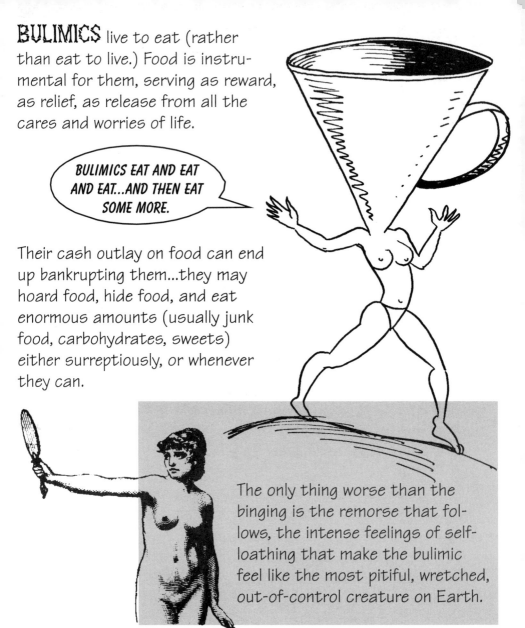

BULIMICS EAT AND EAT AND EAT...AND THEN EAT SOME MORE.

Their cash outlay on food can end up bankrupting them...they may hoard food, hide food, and eat enormous amounts (usually junk food, carbohydrates, sweets) either surreptitiously, or whenever they can.

The only thing worse than the binging is the remorse that follows, the intense feelings of self-loathing that make the bulimic feel like the most pitiful, wretched, out-of-control creature on Earth.

Bulimics attempt to rid themselves of these feelings (and the food that occasioned them) by purging—by self-induced vomiting, which by itself can create significant medical problems. Other bulimics compensate for excess food intake by inordinate amounts of exercise, intermittent fasting, or by the use of laxatives and diuretics.

THERE ARE MANY MORE OVEREATERS THAN THERE ARE BULIMICS.

Overeaters differ from bulimics in the severity and frequency of their excess food intake. The bulimic eating pattern comes to literally <u>dominate</u> the person's life style, whereas the overeater suffers mainly from bouts of indigestion and weight gain.

ANOREXICS go to the opposite extreme. The less they eat the better. Many have serious disturbances of body image: No matter how thin they are, they still feel the need to reduce: they can't be thin enough. Anorexia nervosa can be fatal; a relatively high percentage of anorexics follow an inexorable course ending in death.

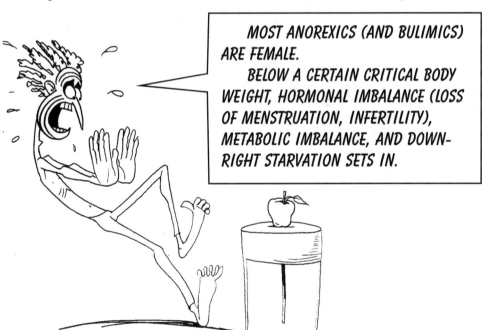

MOST ANOREXICS (AND BULIMICS) ARE FEMALE.
BELOW A CERTAIN CRITICAL BODY WEIGHT, HORMONAL IMBALANCE (LOSS OF MENSTRUATION, INFERTILITY), METABOLIC IMBALANCE, AND DOWNRIGHT STARVATION SETS IN.

The preoccupation with food can be totally...consuming. Anorexics and bulimics may spend the vast majority of their waking hours pursuing weight loss or food or relief from overeating. Eating disorders are often associated with other psychiatric problems including depression, anxiety and chemical dependence.

Sound like addiction? Consider DSM-IV's definition of substance dependence (see if you think it applies to eating disorders):

SUBSTANCE DEPENDENCE:

"a maladaptive pattern of *substance* [italics ours, eds.] use, leading to clinically significant impairment or distress, as manifested by three (or more) of the following, occurring at any time in the same 12-month period:

1   tolerance...

2   withdrawal...

IT FITS! IT FITS!!!

3   the substance is often taken in larger amounts or over a longer period than was intended

4   there is a persistent desire or unsuccessful efforts to cut down or control substance use

5   a great deal of time is spent in activities necessary to obtain the substance (e.g., visiting multilple doctors or driving long distances), use the substance (e.g., chain-smoking), or recover from its effects

6   important social, occupational, or recreational activities are given up or reduced because of substance use

7   the substance use is continued despite knowledge of having a persistent or recurrent physical or psychological problem that is likely to have been caused or exacerbated by the substance

Extremes of over- and undereating certainly meet some of these criteria for dependence. That's why many current treatment approaches to eating disorders incorporate features of recovery programs for addicts (see *Treatment*, page 96).

Gambling, sex, shopping...what *isn't* an addictive behavior?

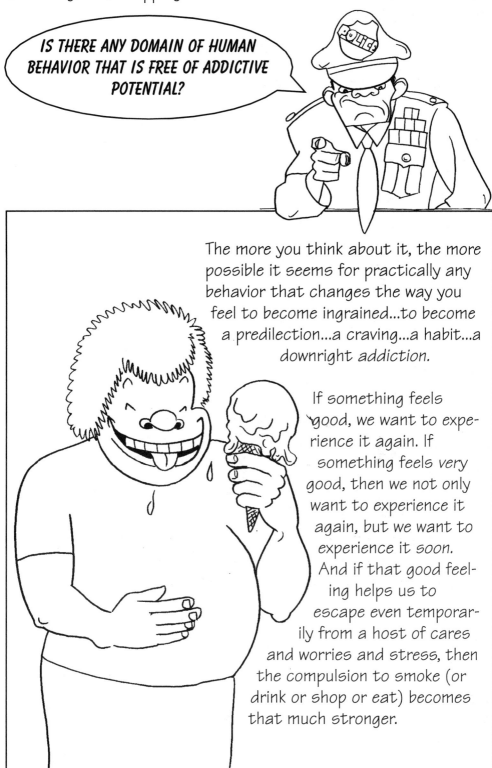

IS THERE ANY DOMAIN OF HUMAN BEHAVIOR THAT IS FREE OF ADDICTIVE POTENTIAL?

The more you think about it, the more possible it seems for practically any behavior that changes the way you feel to become ingrained...to become a predilection...a craving...a habit...a downright *addiction*.

If something feels good, we want to experience it again. If something feels *very* good, then we not only want to experience it again, but we want to experience it soon. And if that good feeling helps us to escape even temporarily from a host of cares and worries and stress, then the compulsion to smoke (or drink or shop or eat) becomes that much stronger.

Sure, people get addicted to gambling (or shopping or sex). People spend months or years trying to recapture that first rush, that first wild feeling of exhiliration. But they never do.

'CHASING THE DRAGON' IS THE STREET TERM FOR WHAT BIOLOGISTS CALL 'NEUROADAPTATION.'

The brain adapts to powerful stimuli. The dragon is too fast—he can't be caught again. And even though they never get quite as high or escape quite as far as before, people know that picking up a credit card or a drink or a lottery ticket will at least to a certain extent change the way they feel...even if only for a moment, and even if that moment then has to give way to

shame,

self-loathing,

and despair

(...and more addictive behavior).

Sometimes ordinary activities become almost indelibly associated with drug or alcohol use. Those who find that a drink or two helps them unwind in public may find themselves unwilling or unable to socialize comfortably without alcohol.

This pairing of behavior with chemical use is particularly problematic among those who use drugs to have or to heighten sex. Many who routinely used drugs during sex find 'sober' sex to be dull, routine, or anxiety-provoking.

Men often use cocaine as part of an hours-' or even days'- long ritual of "mental masturbation." Pornographic magazines, videos and telephone sex are used repetitively and obsessively to focus on particular erotic fantasies, often to the exclusion of contact with real partners. Men who do this report that "thinking about it is more fun [than actually doing it]." Many if not most are unable to achieve erections during this practice, but few appear to be troubled by this cocaine side effect.

Treatment

One way is to ask yourself if your alcohol or drug use makes problems for you. People who experience withdrawal, for example, have a *physical* problem as a result of their substance use: They feel awful after or in between times that they use.

Drug-related problems may be—

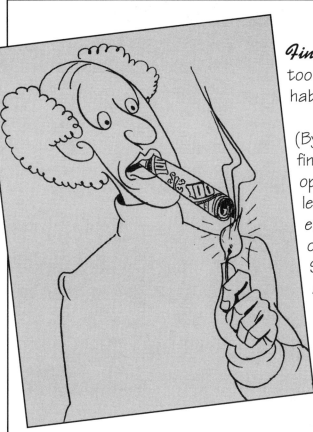

Financial (i.e., spending too much money on the habit);

(By the way: drug-induced financial problems also operate on the macro level. Some have considered the massive influx of illegal drugs from South America and Asia to the U.S. a form of *narcoterrorism*, aimed at destabilization of the economic and cultural life of this country.)

Social (spending too much time drinking or drugging, to the exclusion of family and friends);

(...you can get to a point where the bottle or the needle is your family and friend);

Vocational (missing days at work or performing poorly because of hangovers);

(the statistics on the economic cost to the nation of alcohol and drug abuse are...sobering. This includes bartenders, a group for whom alcoholism remains a major occupational hazard...)

Medical (headaches, nausea, cirrhosis, hepatitis, HIV), or

last but certainly not least,

Spiritual (feeling that there may be far better ways to invest your time, love, and energy.)

A handy tool for assessing problem drinking or drugging are the so-called "CAGE" questions:

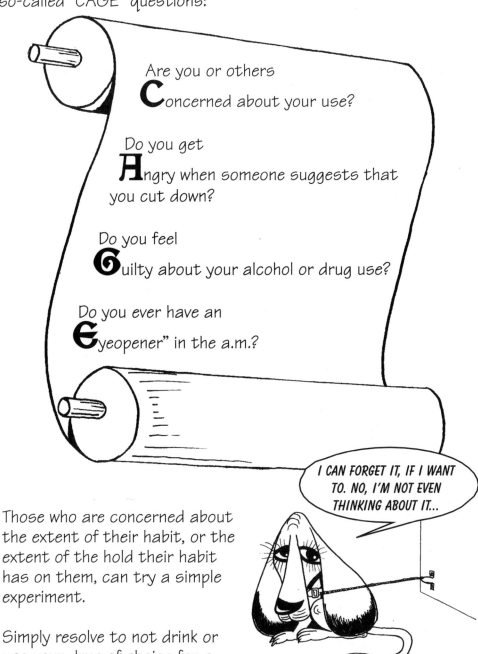

Are you or others **C**oncerned about your use?

Do you get **A**ngry when someone suggests that you cut down?

Do you feel **G**uilty about your alcohol or drug use?

Do you ever have an **E**yeopener" in the a.m.?

I CAN FORGET IT, IF I WANT TO. NO, I'M NOT EVEN THINKING ABOUT IT...

Those who are concerned about the extent of their habit, or the extent of the hold their habit has on them, can try a simple experiment.

Simply resolve to not drink or use your drug of choice for a week (or two weeks or a month.)

If you find yourself unable to stick to this decision, *you have a problem.*

What kind of treatment is available?

Treatment comes in many shapes and sizes (including no treatment at all—"Tincture of Time").

Matching patients to appropriate treatments is critically important. Addictive problems vary on a spectrum from mild to severe; what works for one person could be positively counterthera-peutic for another.

One of the most widely available and least expensive (it's free!) forms of intervention is *self-help*.

Self-help groups include *Alcoholics Anonymous, Narcotics Anonymous, Overeaters Anonymous, Recovery Inc.,* and others. Although the focus of these groups vary, depending on the specific tar-geted problem, they share a mutual inter-est in providing opportunities for expression, ventilation, empathy, and support to members.

HIGHER POWER, PLEASE TAKE THIS MONKEY OFF MY BACK!

The prototype of the self-help group is Alcoholics Anonymous (AA). Founded in 1935 by Bill Wilson ("Bill W") and associates, Alcoholics Anonymous is an international fellowship of individuals who share a common struggle with alcoholism. Wilson, a businessman, spent years fighting his own alcoholism before "giving it up" to a Higher Power and forming AA.

The origin of AA is a fascinating story in itself. As one version has it, one of the movement's founders—still actively drinking—had been given up for hopeless. The legendary Swiss analyst Carl Jung told him that essentially nothing—save for a major spiritual event—could help. This gentleman returned to America, shaken by pessimism and despair...only to experience a vision of a worldwide fellowship of drinkers supporting each other in their common struggle with drink...a vision which in the succeeding years not only materialized but grew to become the enormously vital and active organization we see now.

In churches and schools and storefronts all over the globe, individuals who share a desire to stop drinking and salvage their lives meet on a regular basis to overcome their addictions.

Groups vary in size (ranging from half a dozen to several hundred), in frequency of meeting, and in membership profiles. Each AA group has its own characteristic personality—there are groups of recovering street addicts and groups of professionals—and groups for everyone and everything in between.

SHOP AROUND. IF AT FIRST YOU DON'T SUCCEED IN FINDING A MEETING THAT SUITS YOUR TASTE AND TEMPERAMENT, TRY (AND TRY) AGAIN!

AA meetings are either "open" to the interested and curious or are "closed" (members only). AA members are encouraged to attend meetings regularly; to obtain a *sponsor* (another more experienced AA member who can help guide the newly sober individual through the many challenges of "early recovery"); and to get up and share their stories ("*qualify*") in front of the group. The emotionally charged narration, repeated sufficiently often and in sufficiently painful detail, can produce significant relief from the shame and guilt that most recovering addicts feel.

This is why AA can be so powerful. Relating the story of one's journey through the hell of addiction in front of a group of sympathetic peers turns out to be a vital force for healing.

One theory is that the group functions as a "surrogate super-ego"—the group conscience takes the place of the addict's, the substitution usually being a change for the better, since the alcoholic's conscience is typically harsh and punitive and literally can drive him or her to further drink.

Group support and validation of one's experience is complemented by strong one-on-one support in the form of *sponsorship*. AA members who have reasonably stable sobriety act as "sponsors" for newer members. The key to effective sponsorship is accessibility. Those in early recovery whose feet (and mouth and brains) may still—literally—be wet, know they can reach out at any time for emotional support from their sponsor.

Over the years, the immense popularity (AA currently boasts some two to three million members worldwide) of AA fueled the formation of offspring self-help groups. <u>ALANON</u> is a self-help group for those whose lives have been deeply affected by the addictive life styles of friends and family members. Alanon members learn that they are not alone in their feelings of guilt, helplessness, and frustration. They learn how to stop "enabling" the addict: providing money or shelter or emotional sustenance to an addict who is actively self-destructing may amount to a passive acquiescence (collusion) with his behavior.

"Tough love" may mean putting your foot down and setting limits on the addict's crash-and-burn behaviors.

YOU, TOO, CAN *JUST SAY NO!*

Other self-help groups include OA (Overeaters Anonymous), CoDependents Anonymous, NA (Narcotics Anonymous), CA (Cocaine Anonymous), PA (Pills Anonymous), EA (Emotions Anonymous), and SA (Sexaholics Anonymous.)

The beneficial effect of group membership is not restricted to AA alone. A number of "charismatic" groups (including cults) employ cohesiveness, strong member support and opportunities for ventilation and "absolution" to achieve measurable gains in well being among their members.

For a number of decades, doctrinaire AA members looked upon psychoactive medication (antidepressants, for example) as an unnecessary crutch that was perhaps symptomatic of the alcoholic's or addict's unrelenting disease process. Nowadays however, the mental health and self-help camps have come to some *rapprochement*; AA members now learn and promote the idea that some alcoholics do require and definitely benefit from appropriately prescribed medication for depression, anxiety, and other emotional problems.

Persons in AA adhere to twelve basic tenets, "The Twelve Steps," which are included in AA's **Big Book**, which documents the history and guiding principles of the movement. The Twelve Steps include the alcoholic's recognition of loss of control of his life as well as recognition of the alcoholic's need to surrender to a Higher Power.

Aphorisms like *Take It Easy* and *One Day at a Time* are part of the AA wisdom promulgated among members. AA meetings typically begin and end with a recitation of the "Serenity Prayer," a mantra with seemingly universal appeal and applicability:

God grant me the serenity to accept the things I cannot change, the courage to change the things I can, and the wisdom to know the difference.

AA is non-denominational and need not be experienced as a religious movement. Members are asked to define "Higher Power" and "God" on an individual basis; what is required is an honest willingness to look within and find something other than the individual suffering ego to believe in and surrender oneself to.

AA's *Twelve Traditions* outlines the strictly non-demoninational, non-profit and non-partisan policy of the group. Members feel that this neutral approach is what lies behind AA's phenomenal growth and popularity.

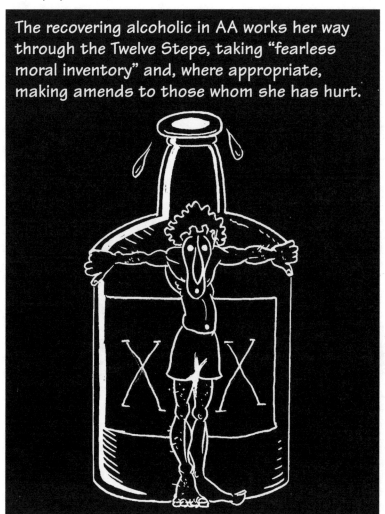

The recovering alcoholic in AA works her way through the Twelve Steps, taking "fearless moral inventory" and, where appropriate, making amends to those whom she has hurt.

YOU CAN START WITH A NICE BIG APOLOGY TO _YOURSELF!_

DOES IT WORK?

MUST EVERY
ALCOHOLIC JOIN?

Because of the anonymity involved, very few studies of AA outcomes have been done. Although there seems to be a stable core group of members who "keep on comin' back," there is also a large proportion of individuals who attend for variable periods of time and then drop out.

Drug use is not a disease, it is a decision; like the decision to step out in front of a moving car. You would call that not a disease but an error of judgment.

—Philip K. Dick, A Scanner Darkly

WHAT ABOUT THE "DISEASE CONCEPT?"

HEY, WAIT A SECOND! DOCTORS AND THERAPISTS TREAT DISEASES. WHO SAID <u>ADDICTION</u> WAS A DISEASE?

THE MULTI-BILLION DOLLAR ADDICTION TREATMENT INDUSTRY SAYS IT IS.

According to the disease concept, alcoholics and other addicts have **an inborn disease** (or "allergy") with

— complete **loss of control** of drinking behavior that is **permanent,**
— which will probably **affect their children,** and
— which always **worsens without treatment.**

The primary sign of alcoholism, according to the disease concept, is **denial:** If you say you're not an alcoholic, that proves that you are!

IS ADDICTION A DISEASE?

Alcoholics Anonymous and other Twelve Step programs (Narcotics Anonymous, Alanon, etc.) say it is...

...BUT OTHERS WOULD DISAGREE.

Some feel that attributing addiction to disease is dehumanizing—that it robs the addict of free will. If we cannot escape the legacy of our chromosomes, then life becomes a fatalistic and gloomy enterprise.

FURTHER, THE DISEASE CONCEPT HAS BEEN BASTARDIZED TO A CERTAIN EXTENT BY TRIAL ATTORNEYS AND INDIVIDUALS SEEKING TO PASS RESPONSIBILITY FOR THEIR OWN HEINOUS ACTS ONTO 'ALCOHOLISM', PROZAC, AND OTHER EXTRA-PERSONAL AGENCIES.

Like it or not, the disease concept of alcoholism (and other drug dependencies) is the cornerstone of much current addiction treatment.

ALMOST 9 OUT OF 10 AMERICANS ACCEPT THE DISEASE CONCEPT...

IT'S NOT A DISEASE, IT'S A MORAL PROBLEM!!

...which, when you get right down to it, is not such a bad thing. Not too long ago, alcohol and drug dependent people were shunned, were considered hopeless reprobates who didn't deserve a second chance (let alone treatment.) The disease concept relabels alcoholics as "sick"; this frame shift opens up all kinds of doors...it destigmatizes addiction and in so doing greatly facilitates the entrance into treatment of all kinds of people with all kinds of dependencies.

CURRENT RESEARCH IS STILL TESTING THE VALIDITY OF THE DISEASE CONCEPT AND RELATED IDEAS.

We do know that children of alcoholic parents—even if raised by nonalcoholic foster parents—are more likely to become alcoholic adults then are children born to nonalcoholic parents. But we also know that individuals born into alcoholic families may escape addiction in later life by a variety of means.

The Bottom line: AA and the disease concept help thousands overcome their problems and make sense of their lives...so take the best and leave the rest. Use what works for you, and try not to worry about the parts that don't. (A philosophy doesn't have to be intellectually or logically rigorous in order for many to benefit from it.)

The disease concept has helped reduce the shame and embarrassment traditionally attached to an alcoholic or addictive life style...making it easier for people to get help for these problems.

THE DISEASE CONCEPT IS JUST...A CONCEPT!

Unfortunately, the more progressive attitudes have not permeated every quarter. Insurance companies are notable for excluding alcoholism and mental disorders in general from reasonable coverage in medical policies. (Hint: Always read the fine print before signing on the dotted line....)

AND, SOME WOULD ARGUE, NOT A PARTICULARLY HEALTHY ONE.

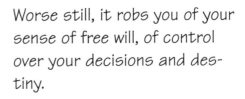

AN UNHEALTHY CONCEPT? MAYBE IT SHOULD SEE A DOCTOR?

The idea that you have a disease that is inborn, lifelong, and that will invariably worsen with time (unless treated) tends to make you pessimistic.

Worse still, it robs you of your sense of free will, of control over your decisions and destiny.

On the other hand, if it helps you to stop drinking—more power to it (and you)! And if it helps you get help...that's good too.

Most would agree that the disease model has on occasion been sorely abused (and if there's one thing that should be clear by now, it's that people will abuse just about anything).

Explaining away destructive behavior on the basis of a drink or a drug or a history of childhood abuse—i.e., "it's not my fault, it's my disease"—robs the individual of free will. And opens the way for condoning or at least pardoning all kinds of unacceptable behavior.

A drug is neither moral nor immoral—it's a chemical compound. The compound itself is not a menace to society until a human being treats it as if consumption bestowed a temporary license to act like an asshole.

—Frank Zappa, *The Real Frank Zappa Book*
(with Peter Occhigrosso)

When someone insists that the Martians or the C.I.A. makes them do things, we usually say that they're crazy.

> THE TWINKIE MADE ME DO IT, THE TWINKIE MADE ME DO IT...

When someone claims that they have battered or murdered because their blood sugar was too high or too low, we call them a victim.

Alcohol and drugs are by no means the only "cuckoo" rationalizations that have been offered for all kinds of otherwise unacceptable behavior. People seem more eager than ever to explain away their feelings on the basis of highly dubious histories of childhood assault, ritual abuse, and let's not forget extraterrestrial kidnappings!

> EVER WONDER WHY EVERY SINGLE PERSON WHO CLAIMS TO HAVE BEEN TAKEN ON BOARD A UFO HAS UNDERGONE SEXUAL MOLESTATION AT THE HANDS OF THEIR ABDUCTORS?

Consider: If anywhere from 15 to 50% of all Americans have an eating disorder; and if children of alcoholics and those who marry or date alcoholics and gamblers and excessive shoppers and sex-aholics also have a disease (co-dependence); then the only truly aberrant or deviant individuals would be those unusual enough to not have a disease!

BLAMING OUR BEHAVIOR ON SOMETHING OUT SIDE OF OUR SELVES IS ASKING FOR TROUBLE.

HERE IS THE LIST OF ALL EXTERNAL INFLUENCES AND OUTSIDE EVENTS IN MY PAST WHICH PROBABLY EXPLAIN WHY I WILL KILL THE PERSON NEXT TO ME...

If alcoholics have an "allergy" to drink (as originally claimed by AA founders), and alcoholism is truly biological...why does AA insist that alcoholics make amends?

WHOEVER SAID WE HAD TO BE <u>CONSISTENT?</u>

Some studies have overturned the notion of "powerlessness": Some would argue that alcoholics are no different from other people in their varying ability to make choices. Heroin-addicted Vietnam vets quitting heroin upon their return home...hundreds of thousands of heavy drinkers or alcoholics (and smokers) who have quit without formal treatment...relapse prevention strategies...all these suggest that SOME people have the ability to "just say no."

I, FOR ONE, HAVE BEEN SAYING "NO" FOR TWENTY YEARS...

117

Other Approaches

There are other ways of looking at compulsive alcohol and drug use.

For example: Maybe addiction isn't an all-or-nothing process. Maybe people become addicted at certain stressful points in their lives and then go on to different and healthier lifestyles later on. Maybe most users are *problem users,* or *problem drinkers:* perhaps their drinking or drugging will not progress inexorably, maybe even resolve without professional or spiritual help.

Different approaches to the problem can lead to different solutions...

O.K., O.K. I THINK MY HUSBAND (OR GIRLFRIEND OR LOVER OR NEPHEW) HAS A PROBLEM. WHAT DO I DO?

You can talk to them.
You can share your concerns.

TRY NOT TO GET SICK ABOUT IT YOURSELF. REMEMBER: THE PROBLEM IS THEIRS, NOT YOURS.

You can buy them a copy of this book!

And as often as not, they will insist that there *is* no problem...**DENIAL**, of course, being one of the hallmarks of addiction.

I THOUGHT DA NILE WAS A RIVER IN EGYPT!

Watching and waiting and hoping for the best is sometimes the only way. As a chemically dependent individual's drug involvement deepens, the resulting changes in lifestyle and accumulation of problems become increasingly obvious.

...and then you...tell him that he drinks too much...

SOMETIMES A FORMAL _INTERVENTION_ IS EFFECTIVE.

This involves gathering together all those who make up the addict's support system—spouse, friends, family members, employer—and actively confronting the addict with the evidence of his self-harm. As you can imagine, this can be difficult to orchestrate. The effort can be facilitated by a professional *interventionist*, who will guide the group through the necessary steps.

Having presented him with the hard and incontestable facts, concerned friends and family then offer the addict a series of alternatives, usually in the form of, "Either you stop drinking, or we will—"

YOU FILL IN THE BLANKS!

HOW ABOUT THERAPY?

DOES PSYCHOTHERAPY HELP?

YES & NO

In the "old days," well-intentioned but as it turned out misguided therapists tried to uncover the emotional conflicts and traumata that they believed were the basis of their clients' addictive behavior.

I'M DIGGING FOR GOLD!!!

Ventilating old hurts and fears is stressful, anxiety-provoking (as in, "Maybe I need a drink to deal with this...")—which are the last things (high anxiety and a drink) newly sober addicts need.

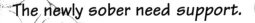

The newly sober need support.

WITHOUT ABSTINENCE, TRUE PSYCHOTHERAPY CANNOT TAKE PLACE.

They need to learn how to cope with feelings. Feelings like anxiety, anger, and loneliness. They need to learn where to turn when their emotions and craving for chemicals over-whelm their rational sense.

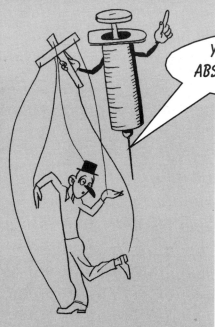

YOU MEAN ALL ADDICTS HAVE TO BE ABSTINENT? WHAT ABOUT "CONTROLLED USE?"

Rarely, individuals who have major problems with chemicals can eventually resume moderate use. **However,** the vast majority risk major relapse (to full blown addiction and all its attendent consequences) any time they choose to "pick up."

Earlier studies by Sobel & Sobel are often cited to prove the contention that controlled drinking is possible. Later re-appraisal of these studies found them to be flawed.

Following six months or more of uninterrupted sobriety, recovering individuals may profit from "uncovering" or exploratory psychotherapy work.

EFFREY TIME SHE LEARNS SOMETING, SHE GOES HOMES UND PICKS UP A DRINK. I ASK YOU, VOTT KIND OF INSIGHT IS THAT?

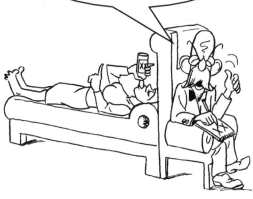

"Recovering" individuals may make deeply important discoveries in therapy. Many addicts, for example, achieve insight into critical deficits they have in self-esteem and in their ability to care for themselves.

121

AA and psychotherapy by no means exhaust the list of *psychosocial interventions* for alcoholism.

Relapse prevention techniques, such as learning to identify cues ("people, places, and things") that set off craving and eventual drug use have been shown to be helpful.

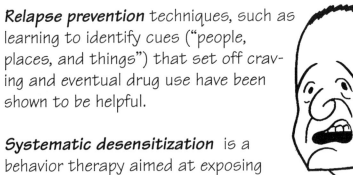

Systematic desensitization is a behavior therapy aimed at exposing and simultaneously "desensitizing" drug-dependent individuals to drug cues.

In plain English, addicts are taught to shut down their intense responses to the thought and sight of drugs.

With *contingency contracting*, the recovering person agrees ahead of time to (usually serious) consequences of renewed drug use.

FOR EXAMPLE, A LETTER DOCUMENTING THE EXACT NATURE AND EXTENT OF HIS ADDICTION MAY BE MAILED TO HIS EMPLOYER IF AND WHEN HE PICKS UP AGAIN.

And there is a role—sometimes a major one—for the individual therapist.

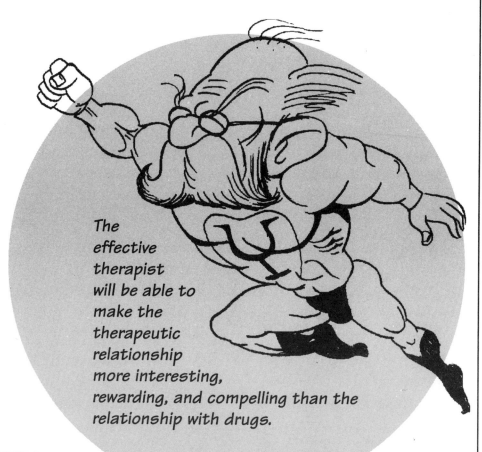

The effective therapist will be able to make the therapeutic relationship more interesting, rewarding, and compelling than the relationship with drugs.

What about *drugs?*

<u>DRUGS</u> to treat dependence on drugs???

THAT MAKES AS MUCH SENSE AS @#$%^&@#$%^&!!!

(Actually, there is evidence that *some* drugs can help some recovering individuals.)

And lest we forget:

the use of drugs to treat drug addiction has an illustrious history behind it. Sigmund Freud introduced his "Seven Percent Solution"—cocaine—as a safe and, he claimed, non-habit-forming treatment for opium addiction... resulting in the substitution or addition of a second set of problems for those who tried "the cure."

I ASK YOU, VOTT KIND OF INSIGHT IS THAT?

<u>Antabuse</u> (disulfiram) is a once-a-day pill that does...nothing.

NOTHING, THAT IS, UNLESS YOU DRINK ON IT.

*NOW THAT'S WHAT I CALL A **SOBERING** INFLUENCE!*

Antabuse blocks the body's ability to break down alcohol. Those who drink while on Antabuse experience a series of extremely unpleasant physiological consequences resulting from the buildup of a highly toxic intermediate compound, acetaldehyde. (Acetaldehyde is similar to formaldehyde.) Antabuse reactions can include nausea, vomiting, convulsions, and even death.

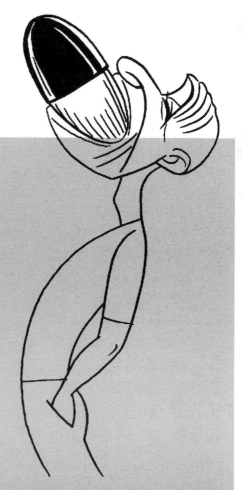

Naltrexone (<u>Trexan, Revia</u>) is an oral opiate receptor blocker. Individuals taking Trexan *cannot get high on opiates.* The opiate receptors in the brain are occupied by the naltrexone molecules so that try as he might, the heroin addict cannot bypass the blockade. He simply wastes his time and money in the attempt.

The dangerous effects of opiates on breathing and heart function are not blocked by naltrexone, however, so efforts to override the Trexan blockade with massive doses of heroin or other opiates can result in lung or heart shutdown and death.

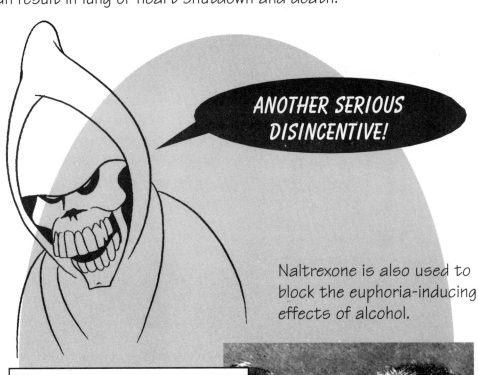

ANOTHER SERIOUS DISINCENTIVE!

Naltrexone is also used to block the euphoria-inducing effects of alcohol.

Interestingly enough, the effects of *placebo* (sugar pill) medication appear to be mediated by the brain's endorphin system. One fascinating study showed that placebo-relieved dental pain reemerged when subjects were given intravenous opiate blockers (which also block endorphins). In another study, joggers reported diminished or absent "runner's high" when they were given an opiate blocker prior to racing.

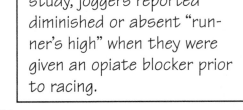

The treatment of **drug <u>withdrawal</u>** is best left to professionals.

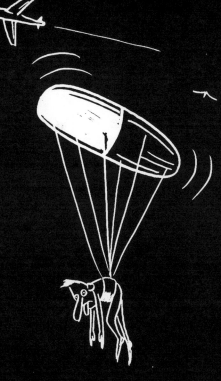

Physicians prescribe *benzodiazepines* such as Librium or Valium to treat severe alcohol (or barbiturate or benzodiazepine) withdrawal.

The idea is to substitute a pill for the substance of abuse so that detoxification can proceed in a medically monitored context. The benzodiazepine is gradually tapered over the course of a week (give or take a few days) while blood pressure, pulse and other parameters are closely followed.

Tegeretol (carbamazepine) is an anticonvulsant that also appears to be effective in treating some types of drug or alcohol withdrawal.

Alcohol and drug withdrawal can have serious or even fatal consequences.

Detoxification often requires a medically supervised setting such as a clinic or a hospital.

Severe opiate dependence may require detoxification with long-acting opioids such as *methadone*. Lesser degrees of opiate dependence can be effectively treated with *clonidine*, which reduces the 'fight or flight' stress response to opiate withdrawal.

Methadone maintenance may be necessary for those who cannot safely live without opiates. Intravenous (chiefly heroin) users are at high risk for criminal behavior, exposure to HIV and other serious diseases, and polysubstance use. Methadone may be a preferable alternative for some. Individuals have remained on stable (i.e., not increasing) doses of methadone and other opiates for years without adverse physical or social effects.

...AND THEN THERE'S PAWS...

Post-Acute Withdrawal Syndrome, that is.

Following cessation of drug/alcohol use, depression, anxiety, and a sense of just not feeling right may persist for days or weeks or longer.

Studies demonstrate that disturbed sleep and negative mood states of recovering individuals are accompanied by measurable changes in hormones and other 'biological markers' such as brainwaves. Up to 25% of recovering alcoholics experience significant levels of anxiety and depression beyond the first two weeks of sobriety.

Untreated, these problems sometimes lead to further use of chemicals. The judicious use of anti-depressants like *Prozac, Paxil, Zoloft,* and *Wellbutrin* may alleviate some of these "abstinence blues."

Psychotropic medication for those with clinically significant emotional problems (depression, mania, schizophrenia) can be a critically important compo-nent of recovery from alcohol and drug use.

The least intensive "treatment"—such as the decision by an individual to remain abstinent—is usually tried first.

If that doesn't work, you take more intensive measures, ranging from self-help groups to professional counseling.

If that doesn't work, you take <u>still</u> more intensive measures—all the way up to hospitalization for detox and rehabilitation, if necessary.

You take progressively more serious measures until you find something that works.

In general, the more that you (and your therapist and your family and friends) do, the better...

...WHY FIGHT THE BATTLE WITH ONLY HALF AN ARMY?

In other words, those who can attend AA meetings and call upon family *and/or* professional help may be more likely to remain healthy and sober than those without such support.

There is no magical
formula for success.
(Except for <u>this</u>:)

<u>Those who want help
can find it.</u>

(Let us rephrase this
to give you a more
active role in your own
healing:)

If <u>YOU</u>
want
help,
<u>YOU</u> can find it!

Substitute other gratifications for alcohol or drugs.

It's easier to give something up if you replace it with something else. The "something else" is different for each person. Exercise, shopping, treating yourself to a delicious meal or a nap—any of these substitute gratifications can end up providing much more pleasure (& less guilt) than the chemical would have. (Plus there's the basic but very real pleasure of knowing that you did something good for yourself.)

Strategize.

Map out your options and plan your time. When not at work or school, know in advance how you'll be spending your time—*from hour to hour. Idle time—and isolation—are setups for craving and renewed drug use.*

Avoid "people, places, and things."

Avoid them like the plague. If there's a "getting high" or "copping" neighborhood that's all too familiar to you—steer clear. Make new friends. Avoid activities (watching X-rated films, for example) that make you think about getting high. Don't go to bars if you're trying to abstain.

CAN I COME IN...?

When craving comes knocking on your door, **Don't let him in!**

Drug thoughts are just— thoughts. *They're not you.* **You don't have to act on them.** If you let them, they will come— and then they will go. Be an impassive observer. Watch the dance of the drug thoughts, *do nothing*, and they will go.

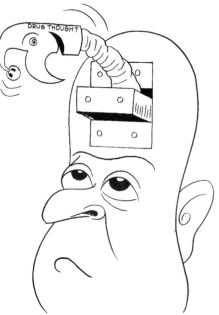

Treat your mind and your body with tenderness.

Health and happiness in recovery are *active processes*—you have to provide the time and energy to make recovery work.

HASTA LA VISTA BABY...

Exercise.

You'll be amazed at how good you can feel. Many find that 20 minutes of aerobic exercise gets their endorphins going for the rest of the day—and end up becoming devoted to this natural high. Exercise *mentally*. Meditation can be a powerful method of achieving the calm and focus that you were looking for with drugs.

Eat sensibly.

Follow a reasonable diet. Know yourself. Too much sugar—or binging of any kind—will bring you way, way down.

And if you haven't been able to stop using on your own,

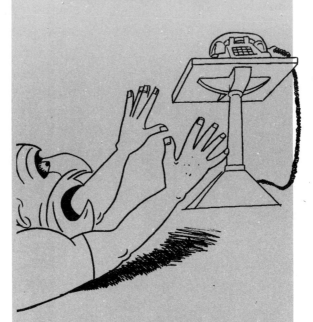

GET SOME HELP!

Twelve step meetings (AA, NA, CA) are available almost everywhere and take place around the clock. They are free and are usually open to first-time visitors. Twelve step meetings can become a habit—and that's not bad. Through AA and other self-help groups you will be able to link up with a sponsor—a person who will make it his or her business to support and monitor your progress in early recovery.

Professional help takes many forms.
Many clinics and outpatient recovery programs
offer a variety of help, ranging from one-on-one
counselling to group therapy to intensive daily
treatment programs. These days, psychiatrists
and other physicians have greater awareness and
more sophisticated tools (including medication,
when appropriate) for treating addiction. You can
ask your physician if he or she has certification
from ASAM (American Society of Addiction
Medicine) or from ABPN (American Board of
Psychiatry and Neurology) in addiction medicine or
psychiatry.

Physicians and other professionals can help
determine if your problem is severe enough to
warrant detoxification or other kinds of intensive
treatment.

SUGGESTED READING

Alcohol and the Writer, by Donald W. Goodwin, M.D. Penguin Books, New York, 1988.

Alcoholics Anonymous, 2nd edition. AA World Services, Inc., New York, 1955.

The Diseasing of America: Addiction Treatment Out of Control, by Stanton Peele. Houghton Mifflin Company, Boston, 1989.

DSM-IV: Diagnostic and Statistical Manual of Mental Disorders, 4th Edition. American Psychiatric Association, Washington, D.C., 1994.

Heavy Drinking: The Myth of Alcoholism as a Disease, Herbert Fingarette. University of California Press, Berkeley, California, 1988.

Substance Abuse: A Comprehensive Textbook. 2nd edition. Edited by Joyce H. Lowinson, Pedro Ruiz, Robert B. Millman, John G. Langrod. Williams & Wilkins, Baltimore, 1992.

alcoholism - definitions vary widely. Typically characterized by a pattern of excess and frequent drinking that significantly interferes with a person's life.

analgesics - pain-relievers.

BAL - blood alcohol level. Measured to determine a person's level of intoxication.

co-dependent - an individual who develops a set of problem behaviors (such as anxiety or depression) in response to a significant other's problem behaviors is said to be 'co-dependent.'

benzodiazepine - drugs such as Valium or Librium that induce sedation and sleep. Can also be used as anticonvulsants.

cirrhosis - advanced scarring of the liver that leads to other severe medical problems. Often a direct result of alcoholism.

catecholamines - a group of molecules that include the neurotransmitters norepinephrine and dopamine.

co-addiction - addiction (dependence upon) two or more drugs at the same time.

cross-tolerance - if drug X prevents withdrawal symptoms of drug Y, then drugs X and Y are said to be cross-tolerant.

dependence - drug dependence is characterized by *tolerance* and *withdrawal*.

designer drugs - man-made compounds such as MDA and MDMA that were 'designed' to bypass legal restrictions on certain psychoactive drugs. More recent legislation has made possession and use of these substances illegal.

disinhibition - loss of usual constraints on behavior.

dts - delirium tremens. Severe life-threatening withdrawal from alcohol that may include hallucinations, hypertension, and seizures.

endogenous opioids - substances manufactured in the brain that act as 'endogenous morphine' (i.e., natural analgesics and euphoriants). Includes enkephalins and endorphins.

hallucinogens - drugs such as LSD and DMT that cause hallucinations.

half-life - the amount of time it takes the body to eliminate one half of a given dose of drug. Used to describe a drug's duration of action.

hypnotic - sleep-inducing.

MICA - mentally ill chemical abuser. Also known as 'dually diagnosed.'

neuroadaptation - the process by which the brain adapts to frequently repeated stimuli.

neuron - a nerve cell.

neurotransmitter - simple molecules such as dopamine, norepinephrine, and serotonin that act as messengers between neurons.

opiates - class of (narcotic) drugs such as heroin and morphine that are potent painkillers and euphoriants.

opioids - opiate-like (*opioid*) compounds which are either man-made (Methadone, Demerol) or found in the brain (enkephalins, endorphins.)

psychoactive - acting on the mind.

psychotomimetic - mimicking psychosis or causing psychosis-like states.

psychotropic - acting upon the mind.

psychosis - a break from consensual reality, often characterized by delusions and/or hallucinations.

rebound (rebound phenomena) - withdrawal from a psychoactive drug causes 'rebound' or opposite effects to those directly caused by the drug.

receptor - a neuronal site that recognizes and is activated by specific neurotransmitters.

reuptake - the process by which neurons take up released neurotransmitter and reprocess them for breakdown of further neurotransmission.

synaptic space - the space between neurons across which neurotransmitters are released.

synergism - the additive effect of two drugs is greater than the sum of the individual effects.

tolerance - when increasing amounts of a drug are required to cause the initial effect.

withdrawal - physiologic and subjective consequences (usually unpleasant) of reduced intake of an addictive substance.

INDEX

I CAN TELL YOU A THING OR TWO ABOUT ADDICTION. I MEAN, I KNOW. I'VE BEEN THERE.

HERE'S THE LOWDOWN, HERE'S THE DIRT: I FIRST REALIZED THERE WAS A PROBLEM WHEN MY LIFESTYLE CHANGED...

I FOUND MYSELF STAYING OUT ALL NIGHT. AVOIDING PEOPLE. GETTING NOTHIN' DONE DURING THE DAY...

SOON ENOUGH I'D DUG MY OWN GRAVE.

THINGS GOT BAD, **REAL** BAD.

SEEMED I COULDN'T GO 24 HOURS WITHOUT A FIX.

BUT I STILL KEPT USING. I'D GET **HIGH** AND **FLY.**

THOUGHT I'D LIVE FOREVER.

BUT THE CURE FOR LONELINESS ALWAYS REMAINED THE SAME: ANOTHER, UM, **BLOODY** DRINK.

THINGS WENT FROM BAD TO WORSE. YOUR ADDICTION WILL SEND YOU TO AN EARLY GRAVE.

149

SUBSTITUTE!

And knowledge, as you will discover in our "Documentary Comic Books," is fun! Each book is painstakingly researched, humorously written and illustrated in whatever style best suits the subject at hand.

MAKING
COMPLEX SUBJECTS
SIMPLE
AND
SERIOUS SUBJECTS
FUN!!!

That's **Writers and Readers**, where *For Beginners*™ books began! Remember, if it doesn't say...

... it's not an <u>original</u> *For Beginners* ™ book!

Chomsky For Beginners

by David Cogswell; illustrated by Paul Gordon

Race For Beginners

by S.E. Anderson Illustrated by The Cro-Maat Collective

McLuhan For Beginners

by W. Terrence Gordon; illustrated by Susan Willmarth

I-Ching For Beginners

by Brandon Toropov; illustrated by John Kane

The History of Eastern Europe For Beginners

by Beck, Mast and Tapper